THE RECOLLECTIONS OF John Mason

George Mason's Son Remembers His Father and Life at Gunston Hall

EDITED BY
Terry K. Dunn

Gunston Hall
Home of George Mason

The Board of Regents of Gunston Hall
Mason Neck, Virginia

The Board of Regents of Gunston Hall
Mason Neck, Virginia

ISBN 978-0-9825922-9-8
LOC Control Number: 2012936543

Cover and text design by John Reinhardt Book Design

Printed in the United States of America

To
Virginia Dawson Beebe

Contents

Acknowledgments

IN 1988, Virginia Dawson Beebe, a direct descendant of John Mason, gave Gunston Hall *The Recollections* of John Mason as a gift to its archives. This remarkable document provides a glimpse into the very personal lives of George and Ann Mason. It is the only primary source available about the domestic life at Gunston Hall. Acknowledgement of her generosity is foremost.

Since Gunston Hall received the donation, it wanted to share this document with visitors, scholars, and Mason family members in published form. Across a span of more than a decade, many people helped to make the first publication possible. I am happy to have been part of the effort to edit the original document and make it available to the public. Not all publications go into a second printing and I am very grateful to be a part of that process now as well. From its inception, *The Recollections* has been a labor of love and many individuals have supplied their talents and expertise making John Mason's treasured document come into the public forum. A debt of great thanks for their help is in order.

Susan Borchardt, then Deputy Director for Collections and Education, first brought this project to my attention when she asked me to transcribe *The Recollections* from microfilm in 1987. Her subsequent encouragement and support throughout the several years it took me to edit *The Recollections* for publication and supplement the document with biographical information was unending. Her dedication to this project, her trust in me, and her professional and esthetic attention to detail set this book in motion. I am most grateful for her unwavering support.

Estella Bryans-Munson assisted me in the initial transcription. Stella uncovered the transposed pages in the microfilmed document and helped clarify the many autographs in *The Recollections*. I thank her for her keen editing that unraveled puzzling questions in the document. Continued editing of the original transcription involved two teams of individuals who strained their eyes for long hours looking at John Mason's (sometimes indecipherable) handwriting. Charlene Bickford and her associates at the First Federal Congress Project gave immense guidance and help in reading and understanding this document. At Gunston Hall, a team of Susan Borchardt, Kevin Shupe, and Barbara Farner (and many staff members who wandered in and peered over our shoulders periodically to assist) helped to determine letters, words, or phrases in the 49 page handwritten memoir. Specifically, Barbara should be singled out for the monumental task of producing a final typewritten transcription for scholarly use at Gunston Hall. Heartfelt thanks to all of them for making this transcription clear and readable.

Also, special thanks go to Charlene Bickford for her reading of multiple drafts of the biographies that accompany *The Recollections*. I greatly appreciated her comments and encouragement.

Great gratitude and thanks goes to the Board of Regents of Gunston Hall for their belief in the importance of this project and their funding of it. I wish to extend particular thanks to Laura Johnson, former Regent from New Jersey, for her energy and interest in making the first edition "come to life" and to the present Board of Regents for their desire to see a second edition go into print.

It has been a pleasure to work with the current Gunston Hall Librarian, and Acting Director Mark J. Whatford. As we prepared for the second edition, Mark recreated a complete typescript of the first edition. My thanks go to him for that huge task—and also for his fresh ideas and perspectives.

Gunston Hall's former director, David L. Reese, took the need and desire for republishing John Mason's *Recollections* to the Board of Regents in 2011. I am especially appreciative that he asked me to edit this second edition and thank him wholeheartedly for this opportunity. It is not often one has this good fortune; it has provided me with a second chance to reunite with John Mason in bringing his thoughts and memories of George Mason – and the remarkable world of the eighteenth century – to the forefront once again.

Last, my loving thanks to my husband Keith, my daughter Chris, and my son Drew who understand why Gunston Hall is so special to me and have allowed me to share so much time over the years with George Mason.

T.K.D.
Williamsburg, Virginia, 2012

Biographical Sketches

Land front portico. Visitors arriving by carriage would be greeted at this classically-inspired porch. CREDIT: DENNIS MCWATERS

Introduction

> *. . . I am truly conscious of having acted from the purist motives of honesty, and love to my country, according to that measure of judgment that God has bestowed on me, and I would not forfeit the approbation of my own mind for the approbation of any man, or all the men upon earth. My conduct as a public man, through the whole of the late glorious Revolution, has been such as, I trust, will administer comfort to me in those moments when I shall most want it, and smooth the bed of death. But as Shakespeare says, 'Something too much of this.' . . .*
>
> GEORGE MASON to JOHN MASON,
> *March 13, 1789*[1]

AMONG HIS PEERS, George Mason was recognized for his vast knowledge of Virginia land law and English constitutional law. They recognized his integrity, his perseverance, his stubbornness, his foresight. He was honest—some might say to a fault. He took no advantage of the opportunity to speculate or profit from his knowledge gained in public office. Most were well aware of his health problems, especially his long and debilitating difficulties with gout. They knew he would argue to put family before public service—even placing the needs of his "orphaned" children before accepting a position as delegate to the Continental Congress.[2]

Yet, in the final hours of the Constitutional Convention in September 1787, when he argued for the details that he believed were essential to complete a document that would protect those Americans "yet unborn," his peers and friends deserted him. When George Mason proposed that he could quickly prepare a declaration of rights that would give "great quiet to the people," it was unanimously voted down. Moreover, one lifelong friend—George Washington—would now revoke his friendship.

Two years after the Constitutional Convention and one year after the ratification of the Constitution, George Mason wrote his son John, in business in Bordeaux, France, and noted the loss of that friendship.

> *"You know the friendship which has so long existed (indeed from our early youth) between General Washington and myself. I believe there are few men in whom he placed greater confidence; but it is possible my opposition to the new government, both as a member of the national and of the Virginia Convention, may have altered the case."* [3]

The costs of choosing independence from Great Britain were of many kinds. Some could be measured; many were immeasurable. For George Mason, his "purest motives of honesty," the sound "measure of judgment which God has bestowed on me," and "love to my country," made his choices clear. In the continuance of that fight to retain America's independence, Mason sought to draft a constitution that would preserve the rights of individuals and protect them from the corrupting elements of power. Unable to acknowledge a document that others accepted—one he deemed incomplete—Mason refused to sign the Constitution of the United States. He paid a heavy price as a non-signer.

Nineteenth-century historians largely dismissed George Mason as a delegate who simply refused to sign the Federal Constitution, but historians in recent decades have re-evaluated his role as an active participant and important leader in the founding of our nation. Close study of surviving documents and letters has revealed Mason's intricate character, broad intellect, and unflinching determination.

Additionally, new studies have brought into sharp focus the contradiction of George Mason as a major slaveholder who argued against the institution of slavery for more than two decades of his life, and yet apparently freed none of the slaves he owned. In 1765, Mason wrote critically that slavery affected the "Morals & Manners of our people." By 1787, he had honed his arguments and rhetoric; he called slavery a "slow poison" and believed every owner of slaves to be a "petty Tyrant." He objected to a proposed federal constitution that did not utilize its "power to prevent the increase of slavery."[4] This paradox regarding Mason's attitudes and actions on slavery puzzles historians. The mystery remains unresolved.

One primary document, *The Recollections of John Mason*, has enhanced an understanding of George Mason by providing insight into family life at Gunston Hall. John Mason, the fourth son of George Mason, grew up and received his early education at Gunston Hall under the careful direction of his father. Close to his father throughout his life, John accompanied him to the Constitutional Convention in Philadelphia in 1787 and corresponded regularly with him while beginning his career in France. John became a respected international merchant and businessman and served a political appointment in the administration of Thomas Jefferson. George and John Mason shared lifelong mutual affection and interests.

In the 1830s, when John was in his late sixties, he wrote his *Recollections* of growing up at Gunston Hall. Describing an image of eighteenth-century gentry life as he remembered it, John also revealed personal details of his mother and father found in no other source. John Mason has provided historians—and readers of history—with a much better understanding of George Mason, a complex man who preferred the "happiness of independence & a private Station to the troubles and Vexations of Public Business. . . ."[5]

George Mason of Gunston Hall (1725–1792) by Dominic Boudet, 1811. John Mason commissioned Boudet to copy the 1750 John Hesselius portraits of his parents, now lost.
Credit: Gunston Hall Board of Regents

George Mason:
A Public Figure and a Private Man

. . . If I can only live to see the American
Union firmly fixed, and free Governments
well established in our western world, and can leave
my children but a Crust of Bread & Liberty,
I shall die satisfied. . . .

GEORGE MASON
October 2, 1778[6]

George Mason worked "often until very late at night during the Revolutionary War when he was much absorbed in public affairs. . . ."
Credit: Dennis McWaters

The small dining room or "Little Parlour" as George Mason called it. Overlooking the garden, this room was used by Mason as an office to manage the plantation, conduct public business, and instruct his sons. His writing table stands at the center of the room reflecting the influence of his words during the Revolutionary period. Credit: Louise Krafft

I have been for some time in Retirement, & Shall not probably return again to public Life; yet my Anxiety for my Country, in these Times of Danger, makes me sometimes dabble a little in Politicks, & keep up a Correspondence with some Men upon the public Stage; you know I am not apt to form Opinions lightly, & without due Examination…

GEORGE MASON
January 8, 1783[7]

PART ONE

Engaged in the Public Business

GEORGE MASON'S BIOGRAPHERS have captioned him as a "Reluctant Statesman," a "Gentleman Revolutionary," or "The Man Who Didn't Sign."[8] Indeed, he may be all of those things. But an examination of his public career reveals a broad picture of political and government contributions that span his entire adult life: it discloses his talents—and persistence—as writer and reformer, a legislator and representative, a militia officer, a local church parish vestryman, a trustee for the towns of Alexandria and Dumfries, and the treasurer of a land speculation company.

Mason effectively began his public career in 1748 when he sought an elective seat in the House of Burgesses as a representative from Fairfax County. He was unsuccessful, but the following year he was elected to a local position as vestryman in Truro Parish, his home parish of the established Anglican Church in Virginia.[9] That same year he entered into a private partnership with the Ohio Company, a company of investors in western lands along the Ohio River. Two years later he was named Ohio Company treasurer, a position he held until the end of his life. Elected to the House of Burgesses as a representative from Fairfax County in 1758, Mason served in the colony's legislature for three years, and then returned to private life.

Only a few years passed, however, before British actions stimulated his reentry into the public arena, this time in the form of protest writing. Following the Stamp Act of 1765, Mason outlined a plan to eliminate stamped documents; in 1766, he wrote to the *London Public Ledger*—as "A Virginia Planter"—to refute a letter published by British merchants who criticized colonial responses to the newly enacted taxation. Mason's written protest statements grew stronger in 1769 as he edited the Nonimportation Association Agreement for Virginia.

Then, taking a dominant role, Mason drafted the 24 articles of protest against the British government in the Fairfax Resolves in 1774.[10]

Mason served as a colonel in the Virginia militia and on the eve of the American Revolution was appointed to the Fairfax Committee of Safety. He helped raise taxes for war needs and worked continuously to procure clothing, food, weapons, ammunition, and equipment for the soldiers throughout the war years.[11]

Mason's skills as a writer and his knowledge of English constitutional law thrust him to the political forefront in Virginia in 1776. In May, delegates to the Fifth Virginia Convention in Williamsburg declared independence from England and immediately called for the writing of a constitution and declaration of rights. Delegate Mason arrived too late for the initial vote on independence due to a "smart fit of the gout," but he was swiftly seated on the drafting committees for both documents.[12]

Mason took the lead in outlining fundamental human rights statements and prepared the first draft of the Virginia Declaration of Rights. Convention President Edmund Pendleton wrote to Thomas Jefferson that "Colo. Mason seems to have the Ascendancy in the great work...."[13] Drawing on his knowledge of the English Bill of Rights of 1689 and the writings of classical and contemporary political philosophers, Mason stated, "That all Men...have certain inherent natural Rights...among which are the Enjoyment of Life and Liberty...."[14] The draft, expanded and modified only slightly, was approved by the Convention as the Virginia Declaration of Rights on June 12, 1776. The new document was quickly printed in the *Virginia Gazette* and reprinted in newspapers in Maryland and Pennsylvania. It became timely model for other rights statements, included in virtually all of the other states' constitutions drafted following independence.

Even as the final debates on the Declaration of Rights concluded, Mason began to compose the Virginia Constitution. His comprehensive understanding of English constitutional law allowed his committee to prepare a governing document quickly, and after a relatively brief debate, Virginia's first Constitution was adopted. Virginia voted for independence on May 15, 1776, and by June 29, both its Declaration of Rights and Constitution were completed and accepted by the Virginia Convention.[15] Mason's knowledge contributed greatly to the speed with which these documents were written, or as historian Robert Rutland notes, "G[eorge] M[ason]'s role at the Convention seems to have been that of a draftsman and expediter."[16]

Mason served as a representative from Fairfax County in the Virginia House of Delegates from 1777 until his retirement in 1781. Then, in 1784, he was asked to serve the public again on a special commission to settle questions involving navigation and trade on the Potomac River between Maryland and Virginia. The work of this commission laid the groundwork for future interstate meetings. As the issues grew larger—from the regional to those encompassing all of the thirteen states—Mason was ultimately sent as one of the seven delegates from

The first draft of the Virginia Declaration of Rights, written by George Mason, was presented to the Virginia Convention in May 1776.
CREDIT: LIBRARY OF CONGRESS

Virginia to Philadelphia in May 1787 to examine and modify the provisions of the Articles of Confederation. The delegates soon found their task to be even more imposing—one of developing a whole new document, a Constitution for the United States.

Mason departed for Philadelphia on May 9, 1787, probably traveling farther from Gunston Hall than he had ever ventured. His son John, then 21, accompanied him. The cosmopolitan manners and customs of Philadelphia were not to Mason's liking and he initially dreaded being detained until July in that city. However, he did not take the purpose of his mission lightly. In a letter dated June 1, he confided to his oldest son George:

> *"The Revolt from Great Britain, & the Formations of our new Governments at that time, were nothing compared with the great Business now before us. There was then a certain Degree of Enthusiasm, which inspired & supported the Mind; but to view, thro the calm sedate Medium of Reason,*

> *the Influence which the Establishments now proposed may have upon the Happiness or Misery of Millions yet unborn, is an Object of much Magnitude, as absorbs, & in a Manner suspends the Operations of the human Understanding."*[17]

When the session opened, the concept of revising the Articles of Confederation was quickly abandoned. The Virginia Plan for a national constitution was introduced and became the basis for discussion. For the next three and a half months the delegates suggested, debated, argued, wrote, and revised. Mason again assumed a leadership role. He was "convincing in debate, steady and firm in his principles, and undoubtedly one of the best politicians in America," noted William Pierce, a delegate from Georgia.[18]

Mason's initial priorities were to ensure that states' powers remain sovereign in the new federal structure and that bills of appropriation would originate in the house of representatives where members were directly elected by the people. He believed that there should be a two-thirds vote among the states to pass laws regulating commercial trade between the United States and foreign countries.

Mason, owner of perhaps 100 slaves on his Gunston Hall plantation, also denounced the slave trade. He argued that slavery in America originated with the "avarice of British merchants." Now the matter of this trade affected not just individual states, but the union as a whole and, Mason believed, it must be curtailed. "Every Master of slaves is born a petty tyrant," Mason said. He added that it was "essential in every point of view that the General Government should have the power to prevent the increase of slavery." Mason also sounded a warning:

> *"[Slaves] bring a judgment of heaven on a Country. As nations can not [sic] be rewarded or punished in the next world they must be in this. By an inevitable chain of causes & effects providence punishes national sins, by national calamities."*[19]

Alarmed, Mason learned that a deal had been struck combining two of his biggest fears—a loss of strong trade consensus and the retention of the slave trade. The "deal" provided that only a majority of states needed to agree on commercial regulation (giving the northern states financial advantage) and the slave trade would not be abolished, but protected from federal abolition for at least 20 years (satisfying the southern states' need for labor and retention of property).

Mason, a southern slave owner who argued against the continuance of the "infernal trafic [sic]" of the slave trade, was gravely distressed at the bargain. While uncomfortably including himself as one of the "petty tyrant" masters he described, Mason was also aware of the issue of property rights involved. He stated:

Couple in front of a Virginia cabin, nineteenth century. Owner of about 100 slaves by the 1780s, George Mason manumitted none.
CREDIT: VALENTINE RICHMOND HISTORY CENTER

And though this infamous traffic be continued, we have no security for the property of that kind which we have already. There is no clause in this constitution to secure it; for they may lay such a tax as will amount to manumission. . . . I have ever looked upon [slavery] as a most disgraceful thing to America. I cannot express my detestation of it. Yet they have not secured us the property of the slaves we have already. So that "they have done what they ought not to have done, and left undone what they ought to have done."[20]

Although Mason believed the work of the convention was unfinished on this matter, the debate ended. The Constitution laid no foundation for the regulation of the institution of slavery in the new nation; the slave trade would continue for 20 years. George Mason remained a slave holder for the rest of his life.

During the last days of the convention, Mason argued for numerous changes and measures. Among these, he recommended that a second convention be held after the states had the opportunity to suggest amendments for consideration, and he proposed the addition of a bill of rights that "would give great quiet to the people."[21] Both motions were rejected.

As the session came to a close, George Mason refused to sign the proposed Constitution, a document that others deemed finished, but he believed incomplete. He wrote his lengthy objections on the back of his copy of the Committee of Style report beginning with, "There is no Declaration of Rights."[22]

George Mason left Philadelphia in an "exceeding ill humour," and suffered a carriage accident en route home to Gunston Hall.[23] Animosity, which took on a political and decidedly federalist cast, built toward Mason in Fairfax County. Mason's *Objections* found their way into print and helped to define the anti-federalist arguments for opposing the ratification of the Constitution. In June 1788, Virginia held its ratification convention in Richmond. Mason attended as a representative of Stafford County (where he also held property), rather than his home county of Fairfax.[24] Patrick Henry and George Mason led the anti-federalist forces at that Richmond convention, but when the final vote was taken on June 25, ratification of the Constitution as it stood was approved 89–79. The only concession made was the promise that Virginia would send written recommendations for amendments to the first session of the federal Congress. Both Henry and Mason were appointed to the committee that proposed 40 amendments, 20 of which outlined a bill of rights closely following Mason's earlier Virginia Declaration of Rights.

During the first session of Congress in 1789, James Madison, Congressman from Virginia, proposed amendments to the Constitution. While the Congress chose not to recommend changes to the body of the Constitution, 12 amendments went to the states for ratification and ten were adopted by December 1791, becoming our Bill of Rights.

The State House, Philadelphia, engraving after Charles Willson Peale, 1778. Mason spent the summer of 1787 here at the Constitutional Convention with his fellow delegates. CREDIT: LIBRARY OF CONGRESS

Before the end of his life, George Mason received some vindication that the principles he fought for in 1787 were principles that other Americans valued and would stand up for as well. The amendments pleased Mason:

> *I have received much Satisfaction from the Amendments to the federal Constitution, which have lately passed from the House of Representatives.... With two or three further Amendments...I cou'd cheerfully put my Hand & Heart to the new Government.*[25]

History has dealt rather harshly with George Mason. Some people misunderstood his objections and arguments in the final hours of the Constitutional Convention as political stubbornness rather than a demonstration of Mason's intense desire to create a document that would promote, as Mason hoped, the happiness, not the misery, of those yet unborn. Some of his peers revoked their friendship. George Washington referred to him as his "quondam friend."[26] But other men including James Madison, Thomas Jefferson, and James Monroe maintained respect, friendship, and regard for his opinion. Madison, reflecting later in his life on the period of the Constitutional Convention, noted that Mason was a "powerful reasoner, a profound Statesman and a devoted Republican." Madison, on his occasional visits to Gunston Hall, found that Mason's "conversations were always a feast to me."[27] Monroe and Mason kept up active correspondence during the last years of Mason's life. Mason anticipated a visit from the younger man that he never received; Monroe planned to visit Gunston Hall on his way north to take his seat in Congress as a United States Senator in the fall of 1792, but he was too late. George Mason died on October 7 before Monroe began his journey.[28]

Jefferson was one of the last visitors Mason received at Gunston Hall in late September 1792. Their discussion touched on the convention and on the problem of financial debt left from the war. Mason had been struggling to recover from a recent "dreadful attack of the cholic," and Jefferson felt compelled to close the conversation sooner than Mason would have liked. Thomas Jefferson paid tribute to Mason in 1821 in his *Autobiography* calling him:

> *a man of the first order of wisdom among those who acted on the theatre of the revolution, of expansive mind, profound judgment, cogent in argument, learned in the lore of our former constitution, and earnest for the republican change on democratic principles.*[29]

In the last several decades, George Mason's name has returned to a place of greater prominence. New scholarship has unveiled a complex man: a planter and businessman; a patriot, reformer, and writer; a legislator and committeeman doggedly persistent in his beliefs. He is recognized as being among those who played a crucial role in the founding of our nation. Historians acknowledge that Mason's human rights statements in the Virginia Declaration of Rights in 1776 formed the foundation for the Bill of Rights in the Constitution of the United States—as well as the French Declaration of the Rights of Man—before the end of the eighteenth century.

George Mason was also a devoted family man. Close examination of surviving letters and documents—particularly *The Recollections of John Mason*—reveal a caring husband and father. John Mason's *Recollections* of his father and family give us additional insight into the private life of George Mason and the Virginia setting of Gunston Hall from which he interpreted the idealism of the English constitution—and helped to transfer it to American soil—and the setting from which he understood and viewed the importance of human rights.

Land front, Gunston Hall Plantation. George Mason built his family seat in Fairfax County, Virginia, circa 1755 to 1759.
CREDIT: GUNSTON HALL BOARD OF REGENTS

I recommend... to my sons, from my own Experience in Life, to prefer the happiness of independence & a private Station to the troubles and Vexations of Public Business; but if either their own inclination or the Necessaty [sic] of the times shou'd engage them in Public Affairs, I charge them on a Fathers [sic] Blessing, never to let the motives of private Interest or ambition to induce them to betray, nor the terrors of Poverty and disgrace, or the fear of danger or of death deter them from Asserting the liberty of their Country, and endeavouring to transmit to their posterity those Sacred rights to which themselves were born.

GEORGE MASON
March 20, 1773[30]

PART TWO

In His Private Station

GEORGE MASON, born in 1725, inherited the land on which he built Gunston Hall. This Fairfax County tract was just one of the numerous parcels of land he inherited when his father, George Mason III, drowned in the Potomac River in 1735. According to the laws of primogeniture, George Mason IV, though only nine years old, inherited all of his father's land.[31] His mother, Ann Thomson Mason, and his uncle, John Mercer, were named as guardians of the three minor children, George, Mary, age four, and Thomson, age two.

Young George Mason received his early education from at least two tutors, Mr. Williams and Mr. Wylie, while growing up along Chopawamsic Creek at the family's home in Stafford County, Virginia. John Mercer lived nearby in Marlborough and probably helped to direct the education of the young Mason children. Mercer, born in Dublin, emigrated to Virginia and later married Catherine Mason, sister of George Mason III. As a practicing attorney, Mercer acquired an extraordinarily large library of hundreds of volumes—many of them on law. As uncle, guardian, and near neighbor, John Mercer and his growing library would have been accessible to George Mason and could have influenced him in the formative years of his education.[32] However, few specific details of George Mason's education are known. Although he neither attended the College of William and Mary nor received education in England as did many gentry sons, his writings indicate he received a broad background in the classics, political philosophy, and various branches of law. His domestic life reveals his additional interests in architecture and horticulture.

In 1750, at the age of 25, George Mason married Ann Eilbeck. Sixteen years old, attractive, and fair, she was the only child of William Eilbeck, merchant and the planter-owner of Mattawoman in Charles County, Maryland. Mason would later describe her:

> *"She was something taller than middle-sized & elegantly shaped. Her Eyes were black, tender & lively; her Features regular & delicate; her Complexion remarkably fair & fresh...."*[33]

Ann Eilbeck Mason's portrait painted by John Hesselius of Maryland at about the time of her marriage reflects that description. Hesselius also painted a companion portrait of George Mason at this time.

Mason began his plans for building Gunston Hall early in the 1750s on the 5500 acres he owned on Dogue's Neck (now Mason Neck) near New Town, an old Mason family home located about 300 yards northeast of present Gunston Hall. Mason most likely planned and initiated the construction of his one-and-a-half story Georgian brick house. On the first floor, a center passage was flanked by two large rooms on the west side (to be used for formal entertaining) and two rooms and a side passage on the east side (for the family's use.) Above stairs, Mason would plan seven bed chambers and a storage room or closet.

In 1755, George Mason contacted his brother, Thompson, then studying law at the Inns of Court in London, to locate a carpenter-joiner to decorate the interior of his new house in a stylish, English fashion. Thomson arranged for William Buckland, only 21 years old, to sail to Virginia that year and begin work on Gunston Hall. During his four year indenture or contract, Buckland designed three different and elaborate styles for the formal areas of the house: a classically influenced center passage with pilasters and a frieze; a room displaying the then-trendy Chinese, or chinoiserie, taste; and the most formal room reflecting features of the ornate Italian influenced "Palladian" style. William Buckland transferred elements of high-style London directly to tidewater Virginia. Mason was pleased; in releasing Buckland from his contract, he wrote that he would with "great Justice" recommend Buckland to other gentleman.[34] Buckland remained in the colonies, designing and decorating several other gentry homes, until the end of his life.[35]

By 1759, George and Ann Mason were living in their new home, as their son Thomson's birth is recorded in the family Bible as taking place at Gunston Hall that same year. Nine children survived out of twelve born to the Masons during their 23 years of marriage. Five sons (George, William, Thomson, John, and Thomas) and four daughters (Ann, Sarah, Mary, and Elizabeth) grew to adulthood, married, and had families of their own. At least 59 grandchildren would later be counted among those families.

In *The Recollections,* John Mason described domestic life and the dominant role that the children played in the Mason family. In "Mother's Chamber," the bed chamber on the first floor, Ann Mason kept a tall chest of drawers filled with young children's clothing—caps, gowns, and jackets—from which John remembered taking out his own clothes.[36] It was his mother's habit to say prayers with the children, and she may have been the disciplinarian, as well; her riding crop of green leather was nicknamed the "green doctor" by the children. Although most

Ann Eilbeck Mason (1734–1773) by Dominic Boudet, 1811 copy after 1750 John Hesselius original. CREDIT: GUNSTON HALL BOARD OF REGENTS

of the domestic duties were performed by Mason slaves and servants, Ann Mason planned and oversaw their activities. Her bed chamber housed a closet used as an *upper pantry* for expensive and imported items needed for the kitchen and house; as mistress, she alone controlled dispensing of those goods.[37] From her chamber, Ann Mason directed both the children's upbringing and the domestic management of the plantation.

George Mason brought tutors to Gunston Hall for his children. First came Mr. McPherson from Maryland, followed by Mr. Davidson and Mr. Constable, both from Scotland; a governess, Mrs. Newman, tutored the girls. Mr. Christian, the itinerant dance master, interrupted the round of regular lessons to teach all the children the social graces.[38]

George Mason considered himself first and foremost a planter. On the four quarters or sections of Gunston Hall plantation and other lands that he had inherited or purchased, Mason grew tobacco and wheat as cash crops; corn, vegetables, and fruits were grown for consumption. Animals were raised for food and provided the raw materials for leather goods, woolen fabric, soap, and candles. His skilled slaves lived at Gunston Hall plantation; most of them worked and lived in buildings or quarters to the east of the main house. The work of blacksmiths, carpenters, coopers, shoemakers, spinners, or weavers could be distributed to all of Mason's properties from this central plantation. Large numbers of unskilled slaves tended all his fields, watched by overseers on the various sites, but George Mason managed the entire business himself, only depending on assistance from "a trusty Slave or two & occasionally of some of his Sons."[39] Mason's sons copied letters and documents while slaves often ran errands to neighboring plantations and one slave served as an overseer. Mason's personal slave, James, attended his needs, kept his wigs cleaned and powdered, and traveled with him.

Mason attempted to be abstemious or sparing in drink, most likely because of his gout, but he had a fondness for French claret and usually enjoyed a toddy, or rum punch, before the mid-day meal. The toddy, prepared by one of his sons, would be handed around after a ritual toast was offered. Following this daily ceremony, dinner would be served about two o'clock after George Mason or one of his sons had said the traditional grace: "God bless us, and what we are going to receive."[40]

The hum of domestic life came to abrupt end in March 1773. At the age of 39, Ann Eilbeck Mason died of a long, slow illness that began during her final pregnancy. She delivered twin boys two months prematurely in December 1772; both sons died and Ann never recovered her health. Her death devastated Mason. John Mason poignantly described the crisis in the family and recalled "that my Father for some days paced the rooms & from the house to the grave...alone...."[41]

Only 11 days after her death, George Mason wrote his will and carefully laid out plans and provisions for his children and estate. This detailed and lengthy

The Hall or Center Passage of Gunston Hall. William Buckland designed this entrance with classical architectural carvings. The room also served as one of three formal entertainment spaces in Mason's home. CREDIT: LOUISE KRAFFT

document required 24 pages when copied into the Fairfax County Will Book; it was never amended.

The loss of wife, mother, and mistress to Gunston Hall left important tasks to be juggled. Ann, or Nancy, as she was called, was the oldest daughter and 18 years old when her mother died. George Mason wrote to a friend in 1778, "My eldest Daughter Nancy (who is blessed with her Mother's amiable Disposition) is Mistress of my Family, & manages my little domestic Matters, with a Degree of Prudence far above her Years."[42] Numerous times he referred to his "orphaned" children; it was from them, "whose Society alone [he] could expect Comfort. . . ."[43]

During the seven years that followed his wife's death, George Mason saw the first of his daughters marry; Sarah, aged 18, married Daniel McCarty, Jr. in 1778. He also saw his oldest son, George, depart for France in 1779, partially for the business of trade, but more critically in search of improvement of his rheumatic condition. William was commissioned a captain in the Fairfax County militia, fought in South Carolina during the American Revolution under "Light Horse" Harry Lee, and then returned to civilian life when he inherited Mattawoman, his grandfather Eilbeck's estate in Maryland. Tutoring continued by Mr. Constable and Mrs. Newman for the youngest children at Gunston hall.

But by 1780, Mason missed marital companionship. In February he wrote James Mercer, "This cold weather has set all the young Folks to providing Bedfellows. I have signed two or three [marriage] Licenses every Day since I have been at Home. I wish I knew where to get a good one myself; for I find cold Sheets extremely disagreeable."[44] His letter hinted of his intentions, for on April 11, 1780, George Mason married Sarah Brent, an old family friend from Stafford County. Mason was 54 years old; Sarah Brent was about 50. She was his companion for the remaining 13 years of his life.[45]

Those remaining years allowed Mason to see a majority of his children marry, to enjoy the birth of grandchildren, and to personally distribute some of the assets and holdings described in his will. Five more of his children married before 1792, with the weddings of George, Thomson, and Mary all taking place during 1784. Nancy and Elizabeth married in 1789. Twenty-one grandchildren provided Mason with additional happiness. There were some sorrows, too. In February, 1785, Mason wrote his daughter Sarah Mason McCarty, "My Dear Child: I most sincerely condole with you for the loss of your dear little girl, but it is our duty to submit with all the resignation human nature is capable of to the dispensation of Divine Providence...."[46]

Mason directed the last years of education for his youngest sons, John and Thomas, and watched them begin careers. John proved successful in his endeavors as a merchant with his partnership in Fenwick and Mason in Bordeaux, France. Thomas, however, caused his father concern. After his training as a merchant with Mr. Hodgson in Alexandria, Thomas entered into business in Richmond, but he soon declared his dislike of the profession to his father. Mason complained that Thomas had a "Fickleness of Disposition, & want of Steadiness."[47] Only three of Mason's children, his sons William, John, and Thomas, did not marry before his death.

Plagued by gout all of his adult life and tormented by "gout of the stomach," George Mason died at Gunston Hall on October 7, 1792 at the age of 67. He was interred at the family burial ground where Ann Eilbeck Mason and their infant sons had been laid to rest years earlier. Sarah Brent Mason, who had a dower right to 400 acres of land on the Dogue Neck property, chose to return to Stafford County to live. She outlived Mason by about 13 years and her place of burial is not known.

George Mason cherished life at Gunston Hall, but in 1773, his writing foreshadowed his own role in public life, one that would be brought about by the "Necessaty [sic]of the times." Mason demonstrated the advice that he offered to his sons:

> *I charge [my sons,] on a Father's Blessing, never to let motives of private Interest or ambition to induce them to betray, nor the terrors of Poverty and*

Done in the exotic Chinese, or chinoiserie, style, formal meals, the service of tea, or various amusements of guests were enjoyed here.
Credit: Louise Krafft

> *disgrace, or the fear of danger or of death deter them from Asserting the liberty of their Country, and endeavouring to transmit to their posterity those Sacred rights to which themselves were born.*[48]

George Mason reluctantly found himself on the center stage of public life in 1776 as the author of the Virginia Declaration of Rights and principal draftsman of the first Virginia Constitution. In 1787, Mason took his knowledge and expertise to Philadelphia as a Virginia delegate to the Constitutional Convention. Refusing to sign that document in the final act of that drama, he argued against its ratification and for amendments to a national constitution he believed incomplete. For Mason, the "Necessaty [sic] of the times" demanded that he fight for "those Sacred rights" to which he himself was born and which he wanted to secure for future generations.

Office of Fenwick & Mason in Bordeaux, France. By 1788 John Mason was a partner in the export firm of Fenwick & Mason.
Credit: Helen Hill Miller Collection, Gunston Hall Plantation

John Mason of Analostan

JOHN MASON, the eighth surviving child of George and Ann Eilbeck Mason, was born in 1766 at his grandmother Eilbeck's home in Charles County, Maryland. John's childhood at Gunston Hall left him with vivid memories of his mother and father. Though only seven years old when his mother died, he stated in *The Recollections* that he was aware of the "awful crisis in the Family" that her final words to him foreshadowed. The solemnness of the experience never left him.[49]

Like the other Mason children, John received his early education from the tutors brought to live at the plantation. In his teenage years, however, he was sent to Stafford County to an academy taught by the Reverend Mr. Buchan, a classical scholar, and also to Calvert County, Maryland, for additional education from Mr. Hunter in mathematics and moral philosophy. Lastly, his father arranged for him to complete his education with an apprenticeship at the merchant firm of Harper and Hartshorne in Alexandria. He took time out during the summer of 1787 to accompany his father to Philadelphia for the Constitutional Convention. By 1788, John was established in a partnership with James and Joseph Fenwick in the firm of Fenwick and Mason. Joseph Fenwick and John Mason conducted an export business in Bordeaux, France, and Capt. James Fenwick directed the shipping of goods from an office in Georgetown. The young business did well, perhaps because Fenwick and Mason heeded the guidance of George Mason to offer no credit, but to deal solely on direct consignments for their American customers. [50]

While in Europe John traveled to the south of France to improve his health and visit Brabant (Belgium), Holland, and England. He witnessed the early days of the revolution in France, of which he wrote his father detailed accounts.

The close relationship between John and his father is evident in the surviving letters. In correspondence during the years John lived and traveled abroad, his father provided the young man with medical advice (both suffered from "convulsive colic"), business advice, news of home, and presents of mocking birds and opossums. George Mason also confided in John. He was concerned about his youngest son, Thomas, and asked John to discuss a course for the future with his brother:

> *[Tom] wrote me a Letter, some time ago, expressing his great Desire of being established in some Business upon his own Account; at the same time expressing much Disgust at the Business & Profession of a merchant; which after the time he has spent in the Pursuit, and which too was his own choice; shewed a Fickleness of Disposition, & want of Steadiness, that may prove highly injurious to him....I wou'd have you, with him, consider the Subject; and assure him, nothing on my Part, consistent with my circumstances, & Justice to his Brothers & Sisters, shall be wanting....*[51]

John's letters to his father indicate he took much advice to heart. Both showed respect and love in their relationship. John's *Recollections* later in his own life reflected this as well.

Fenwick and Mason's first few years in business witnessed great economic change and the political crisis in France. John returned to the United States to establish a branch of his firm in Georgetown in 1792 and the company began to expand into banking, navigation, turnpike ventures, and land speculation. In 1796, after his father's death, John married Anna Maria Murray of Annapolis. With a family that grew to include ten children, John maintained a residence in Georgetown and also a home on Analostan Island, land included in his inheritance.[52] This second home was famous for both its extensive English gardens and the elegant parties given there by the Masons.

John's career expanded over the early decades of the nineteenth century to include the presidency of the Bank of Columbia, the presidency of the Potomac Canal Company, and an appointment under President Thomas Jefferson as Superintendent of Indian Trade in the District of Columbia. In retirement, John and Anna Mason moved to Clermont, a new home about four miles west of Alexandria. John remained there until his death in 1849. It was in these later years, while living at Clermont, that he wrote the *Recollections* of his early life in order that he might give his children and grandchildren a sense of the "condition and manners of the good people of Virginia in those days... but more particularly those of our own Family."[53]

Perhaps most importantly, John Mason's *Recollections* provide a glimpse into the eighteenth century not otherwise afforded to us. His writing captures some of the daily routine of Gunston Hall plantation, the intimacies of family life, and the strong emotional attachment among members of the Mason family. Consequently, our understanding of George Mason as a man caught up in the unexpected role of revolutionary, patriot, and public servant is made more vital and real by reading these *Recollections*.

Endnotes to the Biographical Sketches

1. Robert A. Rutland, Ed., *The Papers of George Mason* (Chapel Hill: The University of North Carolina Press, 1970), 1142.
2. Ibid., 252.
3. Ibid., 1142.
4. Ibid., 61, 62, 965, 966.
5. Ibid., 159.
6. Ibid., 434.
7. Ibid., 761.
8. Robert A. Rutland, *George Mason, Reluctant Statesman* (Baton Rouge: Louisiana State University Press, 1961); Helen Hill Miller, *George Mason, Gentleman Revolutionary* (Chapel Hill: The University of North Carolina Press, 1975); and Helen Hill Miller, *George Mason, The Man Who Didn't Sign* (Lorton, Virginia: The Board of Regents of Gunston Hall, 1987).
9. The vestry of the Anglican church was a lay body of men who administered the affairs of the parish or congregation.
10. The British Proclamation of 1763 at the close of the French and Indian War provided for the establishment of government in the newly acquired northwestern territories and control of Indian affairs there. Additionally, colonists were forbidden to settle beyond a boundary created along the headwaters of the rivers running into the Atlantic (essentially along the ridge of the Appalachian Mountains). The right to purchase land west of this boundary was reserved to the Crown, complicating grants formerly made by Virginia governors. Mason's involvement with the Ohio Company led him to write the "Extracts from the Virginia Charters," a document which provided a legal basis for resistance to Great Britain's policy of non-settlement in these western lands.

To increase revenue following the French and Indian War, Parliament levied a series of taxes on the colonies. The Stamp Act in 1765 quickly called forth resistance from all the colonies. Efforts of merchants urging the nonimportation of taxed goods evolved into formal resolutions such as Virginia's Nonimportation Agreement in 1769. The Fairfax County Resolves strengthened the boycott movement and provided a means of enforcement in 1774.

11. The committees of safety in each county of Virginia were established prior to the Revolution as the regulating body for county defenses or militia. Their powers expanded to economic and legal issues during the eighteen months between the writing of the Fairfax Resolves and the adoption of the Virginia Constitution.
12. Letter to Richard Henry Lee, May 18, 1776. Rutland, *Papers of George Mason*, 271.
13. Ibid., 274.
14. Ibid., 277.
15. Ibid., 274–310. Mason handed the first draft of the Virginia Declaration of Rights to the committee on May 26, 1776. By June 10 he had drafted and presented to the committee his plan for the Virginia Constitution. The final draft of the Constitution was prepared on June 29 and was printed in the *Virginia Gazette* on July 5, 1776.
16. Ibid., 309.
17. Ibid., 892, 893.
18. Ibid., 886, 887.
19. Ibid., 965, 966.
20. Ibid., 1086.
21. Ibid., 981.
22. Ibid., 991–994. This document is in the Chapin Library, Williams College, Williamstown, Massachusetts. Among seventeen points, Mason also objected to inadequate representation in the House of Representatives, giving the Senate power to originate and alter monetary bills, lack of a council or advisors for the president, requiring only a majority (not two-thirds majority) of members of both houses to make commercial and navigational laws, and continuing the importation of slaves for at least twenty more years.
23. Ibid., 1002, 1007. See also, Miller, *Gentleman Revolutionary,* 269.
24. Federalists, or nationalists, who strongly supported the adoption of the Constitution maintained a strong position in Fairfax County in part because it was the home seat of (Federalist) George Washington. Mason did not seek election in his home county as a result, but stood for election in more moderate Stafford County where he was also a property holder.
25. Ibid., 1172.
26. Ibid., cxxiv. Quondam, meaning former, friend.
27. Miller, *Gentleman Revolutionary*, 333.
28. Rutland, *Papers of George Mason*, 328, 329.
29. Ibid., 333.

30. Ibid., 159.
31. George Mason of Gunston Hall was the fourth generation of men to be given that name. Historians have used Roman numerals as one way to separate the individuals for readers: George Mason I (1629–1686); George Mason II (1660–1716); George Mason III (1690–1725); George Mason IV (1725–1792); and George Mason V (1753–1796). This document will make use of Roman numerals where clarification seems necessary. Following the laws of primogeniture, the eldest son inherited all property or title of a parent to the exclusion of all other children.
32. Miller, *Gentleman Revolutionary*, 25–33.
33. Rutland, *Papers of George Mason,* 841.
34. Ibid., 45, 46.
35. There is evidence, both in oral tradition and documentation, that a second English craftsman, William Bernard Sears, did much of the wood carving at Gunston Hall. The strongest evidence, however, comes from a comparison of Sears' known carving at Pohick Church and Mount Vernon completed in the 1770s.

    Scholars now believe that William Buckland most likely planned the elevations and basic design for the interior of Gunston Hall; Sears probably executed these designs. For further reading see Luke Beckerdite, "William Buckland and William Bernard Sears: The Designer and the Carver," *Journal of Early Southern Decorative Arts* 8 (November 1982): 7–40.
36. John Mason, *The Recollections of John Mason,* 63. Up until about the age of six or seven, young children of both sexes wore similar clothing. See Linda Baumgarten, *Eighteenth-Century Clothing at Williamsburg* (Williamsburg: The Colonial Williamsburg Foundation, 1986), 72–78.
37. John Mason, *The Recollections*, 80.
38. Pamela C. Copeland and Richard K. MacMaster, *The Five George Masons* (Lorton, Virginia: The Board of Regents of Gunston Hall, 1975), 115. See also *Recollections*, 60.
39. John Mason, *The Recollections*, 80.
40. Ibid., 68
41. Ibid., 65.
42. Rutland, *Papers of George Mason*, 433, 434.
43. Ibid., Virginia law defined an orphan as a fatherless child.
44. Ibid., 618. Mason was a Fairfax County Justice of the Peace.
45. Ibid., 620–622.
46. Ibid., 810.
47. Ibid., 1269.
48. Ibid., 159.
49. John Mason, *The Recollections*, 64, 65.
50. Rutland, *Papers of George Mason*, 1072, 1129.
51. Ibid., 1268, 1269.
52. This is Roosevelt Island today.
53. John Mason, *The Recollections*, 53.

John Mason (1766–1749) by Charles Bird King, circa 1824.
Credit: Gunston Hall Board of Regents

The Recollections of John Mason

To my Children
and Grand Children

Believing it may be interesting and amusing to some of you at least, my design is, at an advanced period of my life, to employ, as opportunity may occur, some leisure hours in noting down here, such circumstances as I am possessed of, from documents, tradition, or memory, in relation to the history of our family, and its connections, from its first settlement in this Country; together with some account of the friends and associates of that branch, to which you most directly belong; and to connect with these, anecdotes from time to time of lighter or more grave matter that may, in some small degree indicate the condition and manners of the good people of Virginia in those days, generally; but more particularly those of our own family.

Page from the "Recollections" of John Mason, circa 1830s.
CREDIT: VIRGINIA DAWSON BEEBE COLLECTION,
GUNSTON HALL BOARD OF REGENTS

Editorial Note

JOHN MASON (1766–1849), the eighth child born to George and Ann Mason and the last surviving child of that family, wrote his *Recollections* of his early family life for his posterity. Although writing his remembrances in the 1830s when he was growing older, John Mason explains to his readers that he writes only of things of clear and certain memory. He acknowledges that his notes are made "as leisure may happen... and little order in them can be observed."

The surviving document includes 49 pages of writing, most of which is in John's distinctive hand. Pages 12 through 23, however, are in the autographs of at least four anonymous persons. These pages include family and general history; they may be John Mason's dictation to another person or possibly another family member's recollections incorporated with his own. *The Recollections of John Mason* focuses principally on the words written by John Mason and attempts to retain his first-person narrative as much as possible.

The original manuscript is composed of many repetitious paragraphs and phrases, marginalia, as well as crossed-out, superscripted, subscripted, and interlineated words. It is, therefore, the attempt of this editor to give structure, order, and readability to John Mason's document. To that end, superscripted and subscripted words are incorporated into the sentence structure; marginalia are incorporated into the paragraph structure; ellipses are not used to indicate omitted words. Spelling, capitalization, and punctuation have been brought into modern conformity to reduce the use of [sic]. John Mason's frequent use of ampersands has been retained, however. Abbreviations have been expanded. Added words for clarification are bracketed []; conjectural words are bracketed with a question mark [?]. Endnotes are used as needed to clarify words or passages or to provide a reference for the reader.

Robert A. Rutland, historian and George Mason biographer, believed that John Mason was the favorite of his father's five sons.[1] Perhaps it was John's reciprocated love that produced this insightful document, one which reveals the personal, human side of his father and vivid memories of his mother and childhood at Gunston Hall. As interested readers, we are fortunate that his descendants have chosen to share John Mason's document with a more public audience.

Also as interested readers, we wish that John Mason had written more than 49 pages of *The Recollections*. Ironically, his closing paragraph must be our beginning:

> *As I had during my youth, constant intercourse with all these people, I remember them all and... their several employments as if it was yesterday. As it will convey a better Idea of the State of the Family and the habits of the times, I will describe them all.*

ONE

Introduction

TO MY CHILDREN AND GRAND CHILDREN:

Believing it may be interesting and amusing to some of you at least, my design is, at an advanced period of my life, to employ as opportunity may occur, some leisure hours in noting down here, such circumstances as I am possessed of from documents, tradition, or memory, in relation to the history of our family, and its connections, from its first settlement in this country, together with some account of the friends and associates of that branch, to which you most directly belong; and to connect with these, anecdotes from time to time of lighter or more grave matter that may, in some small degree, indicate the condition and manners of the good people of Virginia in those days, generally, but more particularly those of our own family.

As my time is even yet much engrossed with affairs, (some of which not of the most agreeable nature) and [with] the cares of a large family, it is impossible for me to devote any regular series of time to these notes. Thus, they must be made as leisure may happen, and frequently at considerable intervals of time and little order in them can be observed. I shall give nothing here from imagination—and nothing depending on memory where this [is] not clear & certain to the best of my beliefs; or on document or tradition, where these have not been considered authentic in the family.

Mason family coat of arms, ink sketch, circa 1784.
Credit: Gunston Hall Board of Regents

TWO

Mason Family History and Genealogy

[Editor's note: The following paragraphs were edited from the sections of the transcription that are not in John Mason's hand, but are deemed important as they give background about earlier Mason family members. As the reader will see, numerous parts of this area of the transcription reveal inaccuracies; the endnotes provide correction and clarification.]

THE FIRST OF THE MASON FAMILY who came to America was Colonel George Mason; he was a member of the British Parliament in the reign of King Charles the 1st.[2] In parliament he opposed with great loquence the arbitrary measures of the King.[3] He was an officer of Charles's army, and commanded a regiment of horses when the King's army was defeated at Worcester by Oliver Cromwell about the year 1650.[4] He disguised himself and was concealed by some peasants until he got an opportunity to embark for America. He had considerable possessions in Staffordshire where he was born and generally lived (which he lost). A younger brother embarked with him. They arrived and landed at Norfolk, Virginia. This younger Brother, I think William Mason, married, and died at or near Norfolk. Some say he left a son who went to Boston and settled; others say, he left no male issue & his female descendants married among the Thoroughgoods and that family line in Princess Anne County.[5]

Colonel George Mason [George Mason I] went up the River Potomac and settled in Acotinck, near Pastytancy where he was married.[6] He called the County Stafford after his native county in England.[7] He was said to have been a man of considerable talent and great influence in Virginia. A tribe of Indians then lived at

Pamunky on the Maryland shore who were continually murdering and plundering the inhabitants. Colonel Mason raised a party of men in the neighborhood where he lived, came up the river in boats and canoes in the night, surrounded the Indian town just at the dawn of day, and put them all, men, women, and children to the sword.[8]

I think his son [George Mason II] married a Miss Fowke, daughter of Colonel Fowke who came from England about the time he did. I only know [George Mason I] left a son George Mason [George Mason II] who lived the later part of his life in Dogue Neck where he died and is buried at a place called the Old Plantation about half way between High Point and Sandy Point. He had five sons viz. George, Nicholson, French, Francis, & Thomas and four daughters Elizabeth, Sympha Rosa, Catherine, and Sarah.[9] It appears all the sons died unmarried except George and French. Elizabeth married Mr. Darrell.[10] Sympha Rosa married a Dinwiddie and then a Bronaugh.[11] Catherine married a Brooke and Sarah married a Fitzhugh.[12]

George Mason [George Mason III] married a Miss Tompson of Chapawomsic who died without issue.[13] He then married another Miss Tompson, an English lady by whom he had three children, George, Tompson, and Mary who lived to marry. He had three other daughters (who died when children of an eruptive disorder supposed to be the small pox) and were buried in the same coffin....[14] [George Mason III] lived principally in Virginia tho' he once lived at Chickawomsic in Maryland. He was drowned crossing the river in a sailing boat and driven on shore on the beach at Stump Neck and was buried at New Town, the name of the seat where Mr. Bronough lived in the old fields below the Gunston Tract.[15]

[Editor's note: The following paragraphs are edited from the transcription in John Mason's handwriting.]

George Mason [George Mason IV] married Ann Eilbeck, [the] only child of William Eilbeck of Charles County, Maryland, a Merchant from Whitehaven, England who came over in the year 1725 and settled in Charles County Maryland. These, my revered parents, were married in the month of April 1750, at Mr. Eilbeck's seat, called Mattawoman, my father at the age of twenty-five, and my mother at the age of sixteen.[16] He left five sons and four daughters viz. George, William, Tompson, John, and Thomas; Ann, Sarah, Mary, and Elizabeth. My mother [died] in the month of March in the year 1773 in the thirty ninth year of her age.[17] My father married a second time [to] Miss Brent, a lady of advanced age, about the year [1780].[18] They had no children and she survived him.

We were nine children (eight beside myself), of whom I have any perfect recollection. Some were lost I know by my parents, but so young that I have only a vague recollection of them.[19] I was the youngest but two. In the order of age, [we] stood thus: George [George Mason V] married Miss [Elizabeth] Hooe, daughter of

Mr. Gerard Hooe of Barnesfield in King George County, Virginia; Nancy married Mr. Rinaldo Johnston of Aquasco, Prince George's County, Maryland; Sally married Mr. Daniel McCarty of Cedar Grove, Fairfax County, Virginia; William married Miss [Ann] Stewart [Stuart] of Cedar Grove, King George County, Virginia; Thompson married Miss [Sarah] Chichester of Newington, Fairfax County, Virginia; Mary married Mr. John Cooke of West Farm of Stafford County, Virginia; John (myself) married Miss [Anna Maria] Murray of Annapolis; Betsey married Mr. William Thornton of the Cottage, King George County, Virginia; and Thomas married Miss Sarah B[arnes] Hooe, sister of the wife of George. No one of them married a second time. George died before his wife; Anne Eilbeck survived her husband; William died before his wife; Sally survived her husband; Thompson died before his wife; Mary Thompson died before her husband; Betsey died before her husband as did Thomas before his wife; and the only surviving relicts of all these at this day (7 June 1832) are Mrs. Mason, wife of the late William, and under God's will, John (myself) & his cherished wife.

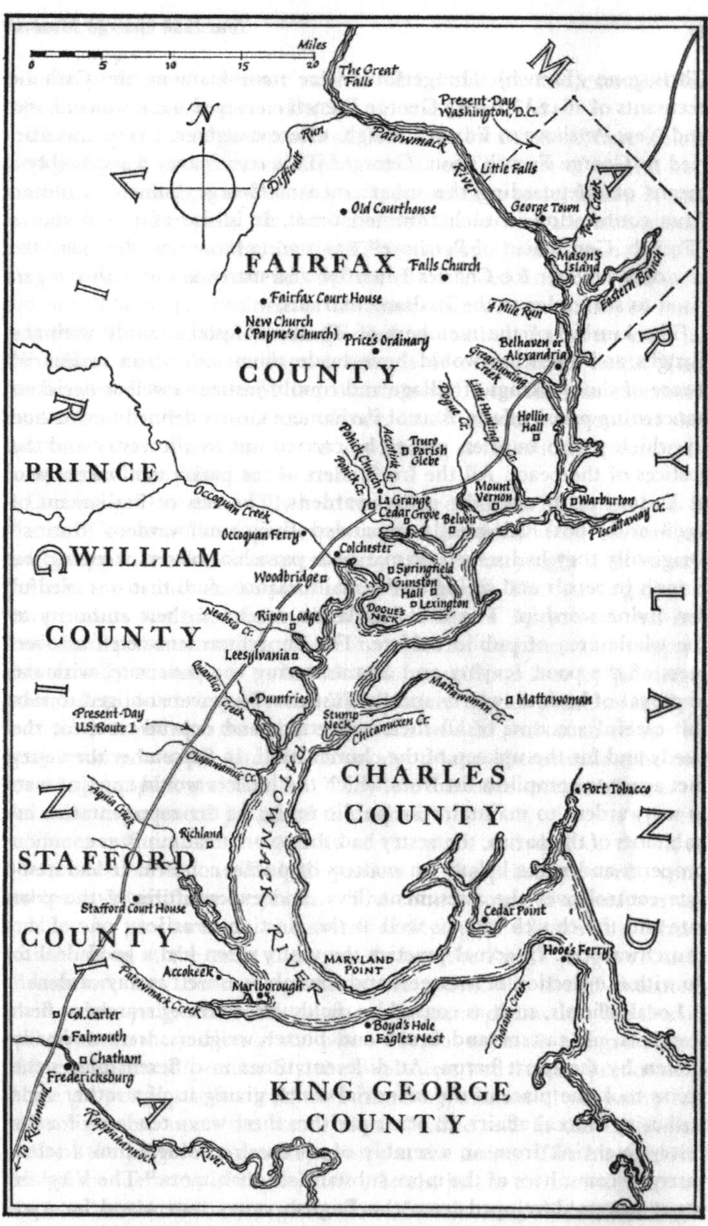

The region of the upper Potomac as George Mason knew it. Locations of plantations (□) and townsites, ferries, and public buildings (•) are approximate. *Prepared by Richard Stinely.*

The Potomac River area surrounding Gunston Hall Plantation.
CREDIT: RICHARD STINELY, THE PAMELA COPELAND COLLECTION, GUNSTON HALL BOARD OF REGENTS

THREE

Early Memories

MY FATHER WAS A MAN of much note and influence in Virginia, long in the public council of his native state and a stern and active patriot during the Revolutionary War from 1775 to 1783. His mansion, Gunston Hall, was situated on the bank of the Potomac in Fairfax County about four miles from the great Public Road from north to south by which all communication—in those days from north to south or one end of the Union to the other—was held, for there was no western country in those days and no steam boats.[20]

At that time, all the best families of the state were seated on the tidewater of the rivers. Great hospitality reigned everywhere. Beside the social & friendly intercourse of the immediate neighborhood, the habit was [for] families who were connected or on friendly terms to visit and spend several days or weeks at the respective mansions of each other from the distances of 50 or 100 miles. Moreover, [it was common] for travelers of distinction often to call & pass a night or several days at the houses of the Virginia gentlemen near the Public Road. During the Revolutionary War particularly, the officers of the different corps of army passing from north to south, knowing how welcome they would always be, very often took up their quarters at these houses for a night at least & sometimes for some days. From my earliest days, I saw all these things at my father's house. His neighborhood was an excellent one in those times, and he was, as I can affirm with truth, greatly beloved and admired by it.

Our nearest neighbor was Mr. Cockburn, living within one mile. [He was an] English gentleman who settled [here in] early life from Jamaica and married a Miss Bronough, a relation of my father's.[21] He was an excellent man, tho' of some [singular?] traits combined with fine talents, and his wife was one of the best women & most meritable housewives in the world. As they made as were a part of our family, and the children of ours—they had no children—a part of theirs, by the most intimate & constant and friendly intercourse. I often love to speak of them and their and hospitable seat called Springfield.

Among the first things I can remember were discussions and conversations upon the high-handed and tyrannical conduct of the King towards his colonial subjects in this country. For in those days the government was designated by "the King" in all conversations—and so universal was the idea that it was treason and death to speak ill of the King—that I even now remember well a scene in the garden at Springfield when my father's family were spending the day there on a certain Sunday when I must have been very small. Several of us children, having collected in the garden after having heard [the talk] among our elders—[of] many complaints and distressing forebodings as to this oppressive course toward our country—were talking the matter over in our own way, and I cursed the King. But [I] immediately begged and obtained the promise of the others not to tell on me.

FOUR

Education

THERE BEING but few public schools in the country in those days, my father, as was the case with most of the gentlemen of landed estates in Virginia, kept private tutors for his children in the family. And the Revolutionary War occurring, and all the tidewater country of the state being invaded, harassed, and plundered from time to time by the enemy, while most of [the children] were yet under age, made it yet more difficult to provide for their education.

The private tutors in my father's family as far back as I can remember were: first, a Mr. McPherson of Maryland and next a Mr. Davidson & then a Mr. Constable, of Scotland both. The two last [were] especially engaged in that country to come to America (as was the practice in those times with families who had means) by my father to live in his house and educate the children. I remember I was so small when the first of these three gentlemen had charge of the school that I was permitted to be an occasional visitor of it rather than made a regular attendant.[22] The tutoress for my sisters was a Mrs. Newman. She remained in the family for some time.

I believe none of [the children] were sent from home but myself and my brother Thomas, who being the youngest sons were approaching to manhood about the conclusion of [the Revolutionary] War. We were both sent about that time to an academy in Stafford County, Virginia, kept by the Reverend Mr. Buchan, a Scotchman by birth, then the rector of two adjoining parishes, one of which was in the lower part of the county on Potomac Creek and the other in the upper part of the county on Aquia Creek, at which he preached on alternate Sundays. He lived on the glebe of the lower parish where the academy was kept. He was a pious man and [a] profound classical scholar. We remained with him about two years. I was then sent to a Mr. Hunter, a Scotchman also, and quite a recluse, who kept a small school in a retired place in Calvert County, Maryland, to study the different branches of the mathematics, in which he was well versed. I remained there something less than a year (in 1785). Thomas was about the same time removed to an academy in Fredericksburg, Virginia where he remained about two years.[23]

In the winter [of] 1786, [I] returned to Stafford County, Virginia to read history and natural & moral philosophy with Mr. Buchan, living at Mrs. Daniel's near his school, and attending him occasionally for instruction and advice and remained there until the fall of 1786. I was sent to the counting house of Mr. William Hartshorne of Alexandria [in the spring of 1787] to learn the business of a merchant and boarded with Mr. Jonah Thompson. I remained with him until the spring of 1788—except [when] attending my father [in Philadelphia from May until September 1787] while he was there as a member from Virginia attending the general convention that formed the Federal constitution.

[In] the Spring [of] 1788 I entered into a mercantile partnership with Mr. James Fenwick and Mr. Joseph Fenwick of Maryland—the latter of whom was then in France—to establish the commercial house in the city of Bordeaux [of] Fenwick and Mason and Co.[24] I embarked on the Potomac in the month of June of that year on board the American ship Union [with] Capt. Trukes, laden with tobacco and addressed to our house and arrived at Bordeaux in the month of August. [I] remained in France engaged in mercantile business and importing until June 1791 when I embarked at Bordeaux on board the French [ship] Louis XIV [under] Capt. Roux, and laden with brandy & specie in my charge [I] arrived at Norfolk in the month following. In [the] Spring of 1792 I established myself in George Town, Maryland on the Potomac in the same connection and under the firm of Mason and Fenwick. While I was abroad, I traveled through the north of France (remaining some months in Paris), Brabbant, Holland, and part of England, remaining in London about a month.[25]

FIVE

Ann Eilbeck Mason

THE HOUSEHOLD ESTABLISHMENT at Gunston Hall was conducted with great regularity & system & I believe tho' large & expensive, much [under] the particular inspection of my revered parents while my mother lived. After her death my sisters being young and housekeepers employed, the interior I [presume was kept] with not so much regularity.

I remember well the oeconomy [sic] & arrangement of her chamber. There stood, among other things, a large old fashioned chest of drawers which held the children's clothes to which, little fellow as I was, I was often carried to get something or to rummage in it without leave. The lower tier consisted of three drawers—the middle and [longest] of these was the stocking drawer, that on the right and smaller was the towel drawer, and that on the left of the same size was the shoe drawer. Next above, a thin [drawer] & the whole depth of the case was the cap drawer; next above this, a deep one & also of the whole length was the gown drawer; next above was the shirt drawer; and next to that the jacket drawer. Then above all came to drawers each of half length which were kept locked and the only two of the whole [which] were devoted to my mother's own private use and for matters of greater value. The other drawers were always unlocked, applied exclusively for the purpose their names designated, and called by all the family by these names.

There were also two long deep closets, one on each side of the deep recess afforded by a spacious stack of chimnies. The one on the right of the chimney contained the current part of my mother's wardrobe and was called her closet [or], as the case might be, by the children or servants, Momma's Closet, or Mistres's [sic] Closet. The other on the left was emphatically designated <u>The</u> Closet. It held the smaller or more precious stores for the table and would have, I suppose [been] called an upper pantry. I can't forget one of [the] articles deposited in my mother's

First floor bedchamber. Ann Mason used the closet on the left side of the fireplace as an "upper pantry" which "held the smaller or more precious stores for the table...." CREDIT: LOUISE KRAFFT

closet. It was a small, green horse whip with a silver head and ring by which it was hung there against one of the walls and which my mother used to carry when she rode on horseback as she often did when in health. This little instrument was applied sometimes to other purposes as occasion required among the Children, and we used to call it the green doctor.

My revered mother was afflicted for a considerable time and confined to her room or bed for some months by the disease which terminated in her death. Long as that has been ago and young as I then was, yet I am confident in the recollection of her and of some of the scenes of her latter days, as well of the furniture and structure of her room and the more so, that they have often since passed in review from time to time in my mind. She was attended during her illness by Dr. Craik who lived in Charles County, Maryland near my grandfather Eilbeck's and who was afterward the Surgeon General of the Revolutionary Army and was the intimate and personal friend of General Washington, as he was of my father. Among his prescriptions for her was weak milk punch to be taken in bed in the morning. Little urchin that I was, it is yet fresh in my mind that I was called sometimes by this beloved mother to her bedside to drink a little of this beverage, which I loved very much, from the bottom of the cup.

The last that I remember of that affectionate parent and excellent woman (for I know by the tradition of the surrounding country, among rich and poor, that she was beloved and admired by everybody for her virtues and charities) is that she took me one day in her arms on her sick bed—I believe it must have been but a few days before her death—told me she was soon going to leave us all, kissed me and gave me her blessing, and charged [me] to be a good boy, to love and obey my father, to love and never quarrel with my brothers & sisters, to be kind to the servants, and if God spared me, when I grew up to be an honest and useful man. The precise words in which this departing and all affectionate charge and blessing were conveyed, I, of course, cannot be certain about, but the substance of them I know I have retained and I well remember that I had intelligence and sensibility enough to be aware of the sacredness of the charge and of the awful crisis in the family it foreboded, that I received it with a swollen heart and fell immediately into a hearty and long cry.

It may be supposed that I have retained a perfect recollection of this scene when I say, as I can with truth, that I have been in the habit of often recalling it to my mind, with pious regard, as well in my younger as in latter days; and I believe and hope, it has had its influence on my course of life. I ought not to omit to add, that it was my mother's constant habit to make me and the other younger children, one or two at a time, kneel down before her sitting, put our hands on her lap, and say our prayers every night before we went to bed.

My mother died in the month of March in the year 1773, in the thirty-ninth year of her age. I remember well her funeral, that the whole family went into deep mourning suddenly prepared, that I was led clothed in black to her grave, that I saw her coffin lowered down into it by cords covered with black cloth, and that there was a large assemblage of friends & neighbors of every class and of the slaves of the estate present; that the house was in a state of desolation for a good while; that the children and servants passed each other in tears & in silence & spoke in whispers; that my father for some days paced the rooms or from the house to the grave (it was not far) alone. The following is the epitaph on my mother's tomb, now extant in the family burying ground at Gunston, written by my father:

"Once, she was all that cheers and sweetens Life,
The tender Mother, Daughter, Friend, and Wife,
Once, she was all that makes mankind adore,
Now, view this marble and be vain no more."

William Buckland designed the most formal room in Mason's home in the Italian influenced Palladian style with its ornate and elaborately detailed carving. Overlooking the garden, this room served as a backdrop for the many social entertainments shared with family and friends. CREDIT: STEVEN BROOKE STUDIOS

SIX

George Mason, My Father

OPPOSITE TO MY MOTHER'S CHAMBER which I have just described and which was [on] the lower floor, but across a passage, was the small dining room commonly used as such by the family.[26] There was a larger one at the other end of the house which was used when there was company or when my father was much engaged. The small dining room was devoted to his service when he used to write and he absented as it were from [his] family sometimes for weeks together—and often until very late at night during the Revolutionary War when he was much absorbed in public affairs and frequently from home (at Williamsburg or Richmond) attending the public councils several months at a time. This room so occupied by him, looked by two south windows immediately on the garden, which adjoined the house on its south front and into which it opened by an outer door and porch that were communicated with by a door and short passage from that room, so that it was in a measure detached from the rest of the house, having a direct and [to] a degree, private way into the garden. My father was fond of his garden and took most of the exercise he did take during the times of close occupation in it. It had been laid out originally on a simple plan both in rectangular walks and squares [with] gravel walks. It was kept with great care, was reduced to a perfect level, and contained, as I have often heard him say, exactly one acre on that level. There were then some falls on the brow of the hill looking toward the river. It was here that my father—in good weather—would several times a day pass out of his study and walk for a considerable time wrapped in meditation, and return again to his desk, without seeing or speaking to any of the family. And in these walks we all well knew that he was not to be disturbed—more than when sitting amidst his papers. During these periods of study the family never were in his company but at meal times. He was always sent for when these were served and nobody sat down until he came in. He always had grace said; most generally he performed that office himself, but sometimes [he] desired one [of] his elder sons to do so. That grace was uniformally [sic] delivered in the following words: "God bless us and what we are going to receive." At such times he was not morose, but often taciturn,[27] and would leave the table early. And I have frequently known his mind—tho' always kind & affectionate to his children—so diverted from the objects around him that he would not for many days together miss one [of] the family that may have been absent on business or a visit to some friend for a week; and would sometimes at table enquire for one of my sisters who had perhaps been gone a week to visit some friend, of which he had known, but forgotten. [This was] not so much so with his sons because he frequently had them in requisition in copying his papers or on plantation or neighborhood business.

At other times and when not deeply engaged, my father was remarkably cheerful. With politicians and men of business, [he was] fond of being ample in his conversation—and with his family and the young company that frequented the house, [he was] unbending and jocular. He was abstemious—and particularly in drinking—but he drank his toddy just before dinner every day, made very weak. [He drank] a glass or two of wine every day, when wine was to be had. During the war nobody could get wine, until toward the close of it, when a partial commercial intercourse with France was opened when he used to import some claret and other French wines. We dined always in those days at two o'clock. His habit was every day between 1 and 2 to send for one of his sons to make the bowl of toddy which was compounded always of West India spirits, loaf sugar, and water—with a little nutmeg grated on the top. Everybody drank out of the same bowl and uniformly; it was the practice with my father, when the bowl was presented to him immediately after its preparation, to say to this son so presenting it, "I pledge you, Sir," which was to say, "Drink first yourself, Sir." This [custom] belonged to the courtesy of the times. You saw it in all good company when the bowl was first produced. The polite return from the person so pledged was to put his lips to the bowl, just taste the contents, and then hand it to him, to whom the first offering was intended. This little ceremony was then & thus a matter of civility in society. The practice as I have often heard it stated, about that time, originated during the civil wars in England, when hard to tell friend from foe in mixed companies. The pledge of drinking first was required by him to whom the bowl was offered—against the possibility of poison in the draught.

When I first remember [my father] he wore a wig, as I believe he had long before. It was [a] club wig with curls at the sides—that is, the straight hair was turned up behind & collected in what was called a club and tied with a black ribbon. He had several of these and one was always kept ready dressed & powdered in a box for exchange. They were dressed & prepared by his man James, a mulattoe [sic] man, who attended on his person and traveled with him. But he always shaved himself, and used to shave his whole head which was covered by the wig twice a week. In summer, for comfort in warm weather at home, he wore a white linen cap often changed in place of the wig. In cooler weather, when he rode out on his plantations or went a hunting—until he was advanced in life he was a great sportsman—he wore under his hat a green velvet cap. His habit was to bathe his head in cold water winter & summer in an open porch every morning immediately after rising—a practice I have heard him say he followed all his life and which he kept up to the time of his death—altho for many years before he had permitted his hair to grow out and [he had] a very thick suit [of hair].

As my father was spared until I had grown to manhood, and indeed entered on the busy scenes of life, I of course, remember much of him. [He] died at his seat of Gunston Hall in Fairfax County, Virginia, on the afternoon of Sunday, the seventh day of October in 1792, in the sixty-seventh year of his age and was buried in the family burial ground at that place.

The Capitol, Williamsburg, Virginia. It was here in 1776 that Mason and other delegates passed the First Virginia Constitution which included his Declaration of Rights.
CREDIT: COLONIAL WILLIAMSBURG FOUNDATION

SEVEN

George Mason's Public Career

GEORGE MASON was a profound statesman [and] a pure patriot. He took part early in life on public business as a burgess in the House of Burgesses of the then colony. He [served] in part for several years when the troubles with Great Britain took [such head?] as to call forth the master Spirits of liberty. [He] was among the foremost of them. As such, he appeared often among the people offering and carrying resolutions to resist the encroachments of the British ministry.[28] He was [a member] of the convention that [sat] at Richmond in 1775 and organized the safety committees, which for a time held the reins of the Government of the Old Dominion.[29] He was a member of the [Fifth Virginia] convention held in the city of Williamsburg in 1776 and was the author of the Bill of Rights of Virginia and of the first Constitution of that State—both of which Instruments were ordained during that Session.[30] [H]e continued to be an active and [influential?] Member of the House of Delegates in all its proceedings from 1781 to 1785.[31] He retired to look after his own affairs and to take care of a large motherless family, always declining offices of the highest station as was frequently offered him, [or] "Declining acting in any character [other] than that of an independent Representative of the people of Virginia."

In 1787 he was sent by the legislature of Virginia to the great convention at Philadelphia for the formation of the federal government where he was an able and [indomitable?] debater, [entrant?] in the republican side and against the consolidation of the states.[32] At the end of the proceeding of the Convention, he declared his [intention?] not to put his name to the Constitution as it had passed—refused to sign it—and published his reasons to the world: because of not enough of limitation on the power & influence of the executive department; that the president was not made [ineligible?] after the first term; that there was no disqualification of Senators and Representatives to be appointed to office during the term for which they are elected; that the power to pass navigation laws [was] without a two thirds vote; and others, among which [were] sternly protested as against encroachments [to] the rights and sovereignty of the states.[33]

In 1788, [he] went as a delegate in the Virginia Convention to pass on the Federal convention and made his best efforts to oppose the adoption [of] the Constitution as it stood and to get another convention to revise it. In that convention, however, several amendments [were proposed] to obviate his objections and were engrafted in the Constitution.[34]

This was the last act of his public Life. But he kept up constantly during his retirement, an active correspondence with many of the prominent [men] of that day. He went [seldom?] out but on visits to his near neighbors and was remarkably hospitable, cheerful, and fond of conversation at his well known mansion of Gunston Hall.

EIGHT

Gunston Hall and the Gardens

MY FATHER'S SEAT, as I have before stated, was called Gunston Hall.[35] It was the mansion house & others built by himself after his marriage with my mother. It was a long brick-building with four rooms and two passages on the first floor and a number of chambers and one long passage on the second. This seat was called after one in England of the same name belonging to the Fowkes' branch of our family there.[36]

It is situated on a height on the right bank of the Potomac River within a short walk of its shores and commanding a full view of it, about five miles above the mouth [of] that branch of it on the same side called the Occoquan. It is now (in 1839) in the possession of my nephew Mr. George Mason, son of George, to whom it was left by my Father, and given him by his.[37] When I can first remember it, it was in a state of high improvement & carefully kept. The south front looked to the river. From an elevated little portico on this front, you descended directly into an extensive garden touching the house in one side & reduced from the natural irregularity of the hill top to a perfect level platform, the southern extremity of which was bounded by a spacious walk running eastwardly & westwardly, from which there was by the natural & sudden declivity of the hill, a rapid descent to the plain considerably below it. On this plain directly adjoining the margin of the hill opposite to & in full view from the garden was a deer park studded with trees, kept well fenced and stocked with native deer, domesticated.

On the north front, by which was the principal approach, was an extensive lawn kept closely pastured, thro' the midst of which led a spacious avenue girded by long, double ranges, symmetrical rows of that hardy & stately cherry tree, the common black-heart, raised from the stone & so the more fair & uniform in their growth, commencing at about 200 feet from the house and extending thence for about 1200 feet, the carriage way being in the center & the foot ways on either

River entrance of Gunston Hall as seen through the English boxwood walkway Mason planted in the eighteenth century. CREDIT: LOUISE KRAFFT

side between the two rows forming each double range of trees. But what was remarkable and most imposing in this avenue was that the four rows of trees being so aligned as to counteract that deception in our vision, which, in looking down long parallel lines, makes them seem to approach as they recede. Advantage was taken of the circumstance, and another very pleasant delusion was effected. A common center was established, exactly in the middle of the outer door way of the mansion, on that front, from which were made to diverge at a certain angle, the four lines on which these tree were planted. The plantation not commencing but at a considerable distance there from (about 200 feet as before mentioned) and so carefully and accurately had they been planted & trained and dressed in accordance, each with the others as they progressed in their growth, that from the point described as taken for the common center—and when they had got a great size—only the first four trees were visible. More than once I have known my father, under whose especial [sic] care this singular and beautiful display of trees had been arranged and preserved, and who set great value on them, amuse his friends by inviting some gentleman or lady (who, visiting Gunston for the first time may have happened to have arrived after night, or may have come by way of the river and entered by the other front and so not have seen the avenue) to the north front to see the grounds. And then by placing them exactly in the middle of the door way and asking, "How many trees do you see before you?" "Four," would necessarily be the answer, because, the fact was, that those at the end of the four rows next [to] the house, completely—and especially when in full leaf—concealed from that view, body & top, all the others, tho' more than fifty in each row. Then came the request, "Be good enough to place yourself now close to either side of the door way & then tell us how many you see." The answer would now be with delight and surprise, but as necessarily, "A great number, and to a vast extent, but how many it is impossible to say!" And in truth, to the eye placed at only about two feet to the right or left of the first position, there were presented, as if by magic, four long and apparently close walls of wood, made up of the bodies of the trees, and above as many of rich foliage constituted by their boughs stretching as seemed to an immeasurable distance.[38]

To the west of the main building were first the school house and then, at a little distance, masqued by a row of large English walnut trees, were the stables. To the east was a high paled yard, adjoining the house, into which opened an outer door from the private front, within or connected with which yard were the kitchen, well, poultry houses, and other domestic arrangements. And beyond it on the same side were the corn house and grainery, servant houses (in them [sic] days called Negroe [sic] quarters), hay yard & cattle pens, all of which [were] masqued by rows of large cherry and mulberry trees. And adjoining the enclosed grounds on which stood the mansion and all these appendages in the eastern side was an extensive pasture for stock of all kinds, running down to the river, through which led the road to the Landing, emphatically so called, where all persons or things water borne, were landed or taken off, and where were kept the boats, pettiaugers, and canoes, of which there were always several for business transportation, fishing, and hunting, belonging to the establishment.[39] Farther north & on the same side was an extensive orchard of fine fruit trees & of a variety of kinds. Beyond this was a small & highly fenced pasture devoted to a single brood horse. The occupant, I recollect in my early days, was named Vulcan, of the best stock in the country, and a direct descendant of the celebrated old Janus.[40]

The north west side of the lawn or enclosed ground was skirted by a wood, just far enough within which, to be out of sight, was a little village called Log-Town, so called because most of the houses were built of hewn pine logs. Here lived several families of the slaves serving about the mansion house. Among them were my father's body servant, James, a mulattoe [sic] man & his family, and those of several Negro carpenters.

The heights on which the mansion house stood extended in an east and west direction across an isthmus and were at he northern extremity of the estate to which it belonged. This contained something more than five thousand acres and was called Dogue's Neck, (I believe after the tribe of Indians which had inhabited

Reconstructed schoolhouse. One of over 30 buildings on Geoerge Mason's plantation, the schoolhouse served as both home and work place for the family's tutor. CREDIT: DENNIS McWATERS

these and the neighboring country), water-locked by the Potomac on the south, by the Occoquan on the west, and Pohick Creek (a bold & navigable branch of the Potomac) on the east, and again by Holt's Creek, a branch of the Occoquan that stretches for some distance across from that river in an easterly direction. The isthmus on the northern boundary is narrow and the whole estate was kept completely enclosed by a fence on that side of about one mile in length, running from the head of Holt's to the margin of Pohick Creek. This fence was maintained with great care & in good repair in my father's time in order to secure his own stock the exclusive range within it and made of uncommon height to keep in the native deer, which had been preserved there in abundance from the first settlement of the country—and indeed are yet there in considerable numbers. The land south of the heights comprising more than nine tenths of the estate was an [sic] uniform level elevated some twenty feet above the surface of the river, with the exception of one extensive marsh & three or four water courses which were accompanied by some ravines and undulations of minor character. About two thirds of it were yet clothed with the primate wood; the whole of this level tract was embraced in one view from the mansion house. In different parts of this tract and detached from each other, my Father worked four plantations with his own slaves, each under an overseer, and containing 4 or 500 acres of open land.[41] His crops were principally Indian corn and tobacco, the corn for the support of the plantation and the home-house and the tobacco for sale. There was but little small grain made in that part of the country in those days.[42] He had another plantation worked in the same manner on an estate he had in Charles County, Maryland on the Potomac, about twenty miles lower down at a place called Stump Neck.

Land front porch of Gunston Hall c. 1870. Across two centuries, first as enslaved peoples – and later as freedmen and women – African Virginians worked about the house and plantation of Gunston Hall.
Credit: Gunston Hall Plantation

NINE

Slaves

IT WAS VERY MUCH the practice with gentlemen of landed & slave estates on the interior of Virginia, so to organize them, as to have considerable resources within themselves; to employ, or pay, but few tradesmen & buy little or none of the course stuffs and materials used by them; and this practice became stronger and more general during the long period of the Revolutionary War which in great measure cut off the means of supply from else where.

Thus my father had among his slaves: carpenters, coopers, sawyers, blacksmiths, tanners, curriers, shoemakers, spinners, weavers & knitters, and even a distiller. His woods furnished timber and plank for the carpenters and coopers and charcoal for the blacksmith; his cattle killed for his own consumption or for sale, supplied skins for the tanners, curriers & shoemakers; and his sheep gave wool and his fields produced cotton and flax for the weavers and spinners; and his orchards fruit for the distiller. His carpenters & sawyers built and kept in repair all the dwelling houses, barns, stables, ploughs, harrows, gates, &c. on the plantations & the out houses at the home house. His coopers made the hogsheads the tobacco was prized in, and the tight casks to hold the cyder & other liquors. The tanners and curriers with the proper vats &c, tanned & dressed the skins as well for upper as for soul [sic] leather to the full amount of the consumption of the estate and the shoemakers made them into shoes for the Negroes. A professional shoemaker was hired for 3 or 4 months in the year to come and make up the shoes for the white part of the family. The blacksmith did all the iron work required by the establishment such as making & repairing ploughs, harrows, teeth, chains, bolts, &c., &c. The spinners, weavers, & knitters made all the coarse cloth & stockings used by Negroes and some of the finer texture worn by the white family—nearly all worn by the children of it. The distiller made every fall a good deal of apple, peach, and persimmon brandy. The art of distilling from grain was not then among us...but [at a] few public distilleries. All these operations were carried on at the home house and their results distributed as occasion required to the different plantations. Moreover, all the Beeves [sic] and hogs for consumption or sale were driven up and slaughtered there at the proper seasons, and whatever was to be preserved was to be salted & packed away for after distribution.

My father kept no stewart [sic] or clerk about him.[43] He kept his own books and superintended, with the assistance of a trusty slave or two, & occasionally some of his sons, all the operations at or about the home house just above described, except that during the Revolutionary War & when it was necessary to do a great deal in that way to clothe all his slaves, he had in his service, a white man, a weaver of the finer stuffs, to weave himself and superintend the black weavers, and a white woman to superintend the Negroe [sic] spinning women. To carry on these operations to the extent required, it will be seen that a considerable force was necessary beside the house servants who, for such a household—a large family & entertaining a great deal of company—must be numerous. And such a force was constantly kept independently of any [of] the plantations and beside occasional drafts from them of labour for particular occasions.

TEN

Epilogue

WE, THE CHILDREN, all lived together in great harmony at the paternal mansion until the respective periods arrived when each by marriage, or pursuits in business for themselves, were successively drawn off from that common home. And I can add with truth, as I do with infinite pleasure, and as a just tribute to the memory of my brothers and sisters, all of whom have now for some years departed this life, that the most sincere, constant affection and interchange of kindly offices subsisted afterwards among us all, during the whole period of their lives; and that there never was, to the best of my knowledge, a single quarrel or even a transient coolness that ever took place between any of us.

Endnotes to *The Recollections of John Mason*

1. Robert A. Rutland, Ed., *The Papers of George Mason* (Chapel Hill: The University of North Carolina Press, 1970), 695.
2. Historians have used Roman numerals as one way to separate the individuals similarly named George Mason in this family: George Mason I (1629–1686); George Mason II (1660–1716); George Mason III (1690–1735); George Mason IV (1725–1792); and George Mason V (1753–1796). This document will use Roman numerals where clarification seems necessary.
3. Loquence—speech or discourse.
4. Biographer Kate Mason Rowland states that published records of the members of British Parliament do not include George Mason. See Kate Mason Rowland, *The Life of George Mason* (New York: Russell and Russell, Inc., 1964), 3. Strong family tradition maintains that George Mason I was a royalist colonel, defeated at the second battle of Worchester in 1651. His name is not listed on preserved military rolls, however. See Rowland, ibid. and also Pamela C. Copeland and Richard K. MacMaster, *The Five George Masons* (Lorton, VA: Board of Regents of Gunston Hall, 1975), 9–12.
5. Current Mason genealogical research does not confirm this family history of William Mason. However, records of the English Civil War period are incomplete and additional study of surviving sources needs to be done. Personal conversation with Genevieve Jones, Gunston Hall Genealogist.
6. The name of the plantation where George Mason I lived and died was Accokeek.
7. George Mason I is believed to have been born in Staffordshire, England. See Rowland, *Life of George Mason*, 2.
8. George Mason I was the commanding officer of the Stafford County, Virginia militia in the 1660s when relations worsened between English and Native American

neighbors. Virginia and Maryland militia committed a brutal murder of four Susquehannock Indian tribe superiors (sachems) in 1675. The Indian's defense of the Piscataway Fort in Maryland withstood a six week siege, but an Indian war party subsequently escaped and passed through English lines and crossed the Potomac River into Virginia committing many brutal acts of violence. When the warring Susquehannocks reached the fall line of the James River, they killed Nathaniel Bacon's overseer and one of his servants. As a leader of frontiersmen, Bacon warred on friendly and neutral Indian tribes, not just hostile Indians. Although George Mason I may have participated in the Piscataway Fort incident, he played no further role in Bacon's Rebellion. See Copeland and MacMaster, *The Five George Masons*, 11–17.

9. George Mason II married three times, first: Mary Fowke; second, Elizabeth Waugh; and third, Sarah Taliaferro. He had a total of twelve children, six sons, (including Gerard) and six daughters (including Mary and Ann).
10. Elizabeth Mason married William Roy.
11. Sympha Rosa Ann Field Mason first married John Dinwiddie, brother of Virginia's Lieutenant Governor Robert Dinwiddie (1752–1758) and, subsequently, she married Jeremiah Bronaugh. Copeland and MacMaster, *The Five George Masons*, 48.
12. Catherine married John Mercer. Sarah married three times: first, Thomas Brook; second, Roger Chamberlain; and third, Francis M. Mastin. Ann married three times: first, William Darrall; second, Thomas Fitzhugh; and third, Thomas Smith. Mary married George Fitzhugh and then Benjamin Strother. See note 9 above, also.
13. No documentation supports or disproves this statement of a first marriage to this Miss Tompson. There was a Thomson family living in Stafford County, Virginia, however. Personal conversation with Genevieve Jones, Gunston Hall Genealogist. Note: the manuscript used various spellings of Tomson, Thompson, and Thomson.
14. This ellipsis is in the manuscript text and is not an editorial mark. George Mason III married Ann Thomson, daughter of Stevens Thomson, in 1721. Stevens Thomson had been the attorney general for Governor Francis Nicholson. See Copeland and MacMaster, *The Five George Masons*, 54, 55.
15. Newtown or New Town was the Mason family home on Pohick Creek, located about 300 yards northeast of the present Gunston Hall. The above paragraphs on family history are written in unknown autographs.
16. George Mason and Ann Eilbeck were married on April 4, 1750 in Charles County, Maryland. The ceremony was performed by Mason's close friend, the Reverend John Moncure. The *Maryland Gazette* reported the marriage on May 2, 1750, describing the bride as "a young lady of distinguished merits and beauty and a handsome fortune." See Copeland and MacMaster, *The Five George Masons*, 90.
17. Three of the Mason daughters had nicknames: Ann was called "Nancy;" Sarah was called "Sally;" and Elizabeth was called "Betsey." See the Genealogy Chart on page 73. Ann Eilbeck Mason died at Gunston Hall on March 9, 1773.

18. There is no year written in the blank space in *The Recollections* for the marriage of Sarah Brent and George Mason, but the marriage took place on April 11, 1780 in Prince William County, Virginia. They were married by Mason's long-time friend, the Reverend James Scott.
19. Three children died in infancy: William (1756–1757) and twins, Richard and James (1772), who died several months before the death of Ann Eilbeck Mason.
20. The Great Public Road, or King's Highway, became U.S. Route 1. Potomac is spelled variously as Potomok, Potomack, Potomak, and Potomac throughout John Mason's writing. It is spelled in the current convention, Potomac, in *The Recollections*.
21. Martin Cockburn was born in Jamaica, married Ann Bronaugh in 1735 (cousin to George Mason IV), and lived at Springfield, the adjoining plantation to Gunston Hall.
22. In a separate "Short Narrative," John Mason writes: "I was educated at Gunston Hall…by private teachers…with my brothers and a few Young Gentlemen, the sons of my father's Friends in the neighborhood, who were permitted by my Father to come as day scholars to these Tutors who resided in his family about the year 1781 or 1782. Mr[.] Constable having left the Family during the revolutionary war I was kept at home without a Teacher untill [sic] the Spring of 1783." Unpublished paper, Gunston Hall Library. George Mason had requested Mr. Constable's safe passage to the West Indies from Virginia Governor Thomas Nelson in 1781. See Rutland, *Papers of George Mason*, 695, 696.
23. Thomas Mason and George Graham (nephew of Sarah Brent Mason who came to live at Gunston Hall with his aunt) both attended Fredericksburg Academy. See Copeland and MacMaster, *The Five George Masons*, 243.
24. James and Joseph Fenwick were brothers. James, a ship's captain, directed his transatlantic business from the Potomac region. George Mason IV was a major customer. Joseph Fenwick had established himself as an independent merchant in Bordeaux, France in 1787 and went into partnership with John Mason in 1788. George Mason recommended Joseph Fenwick to President George Washington for the position of American consul in Bordeaux; he received that appointment and served in the post from 1790–1798. See Copeland and MacMaster, *The Five George Masons*, 247–251.
25. John Mason apparently made two extensive trips while living in France. The first one to northern parts of Europe took place from February to June in 1789. He also visited the south of France sometime in 1790–1791: Montaubon, Toulouse, Carcassone, Montpelier, Marseilles, Hieres, Avignon, and Nimmes. Unpublished paper, Gunston Hall Library. Specie—hard currency; coins of gold and silver.
26. This is the room George Mason called the "little Parlour." See Rutland, *Papers of George Mason*, 893.
27. Taciturn—reserved, disinclined to conversation.

28. George Mason served as an elected Burgess to the House of Burgesses from 1758 to 1761 from Fairfax County. In 1769 he edited the Nonimportation Association Agreement for Virginia and in 1774 he drafted the Fairfax Resolves protesting British parliamentary policies against the colonies.
29. In May, 1774, Virginia's Royal Governor, Lord Dunmore, dissolved the House of Burgesses after the House proposed holding a day of fasting in response to the closing of the port of Boston following the infamous "tea party." The Burgesses immediately reconvened at the Raleigh Tavern (now calling themselves an Association), to plan their fasting day and to issue a call for a Continental Congress; they subsequently called for a convention in August to discuss plans for a boycott. The August convention became the first of five Virginia Conventions, the final one taking place in May, 1776 when independence from Great Britain was declared. George Mason served as a delegate beginning with the Third Virginia Convention; he was elected to fill the seat vacated by George Washington after he was named Commanding General of the Continental Army. The Third Convention met in Richmond in July and August, 1775. The Third Convention approved a Committee of Safety; primarily an executive board for the Virginia military, it also became a body for legal enforcement before a constitution was drafted and a legitimate government was set up in Virginia. George Mason was appointed to the Committee of Safety.
30. Immediately following the Fifth Virginia Convention's unanimous vote for independence from Great Britain on May 15, 1776, committees were established to draft a constitution and declaration of rights. Mason arrived after the vote (due to an attack of gout), but in time to be appointed to both committees. Mason's writing, with slight modification, formed the basis for the 16 points of the Virginia Declaration of Rights adopted on June 12, 1776. Mason also provided the draft for the first Virginia Constitution which was approved with limited change on June 29, 1776. George Mason's vast knowledge of English constitutional law and his profound belief in fundamental human rights placed him at the forefront of this convention as a draftsman and expediter of these two documents. See Rutland, *Papers of George Mason*, 309.
31. The dates in the manuscript are transposed—and are incorrect. Mason served in the Virginia House of Delegates as an elected representative from Fairfax County from 1777 until 1781, and then retired.
32. Mason served on the Virginia-Maryland commission that addressed questions of trade on the Potomac River in 1784. Ultimately, this commission evolved into the Constitutional Convention that met in Philadelphia in 1787. Mason was one of seven appointed delegates from Virginia to that Convention.
33. Mason's objections to the federal constitution began with "There is no Declaration of Rights..." and encompassed sixteen paragraphs. Mason distributed these objections to friends, but they found their way into print without his "Approbation,

or Privity." They ultimately formed the basis for the Antifederalist arguments. See Appendix. See also Rutland, *Papers of George Mason*, 993, 994.

34. Mason was elected as a delegate from Stafford County to the Ratification Convention held in Richmond in 1788. George Mason and Patrick Henry argued strenuously against ratification of the Constitution as it stood, but lost by a vote of 89–79. However, a committee was formed to draft subsequent amendments; both Mason and Henry served on that committee. Of 40 suggested amendments, half included human rights statements taken largely from the Virginia Declaration of Rights of 1776. Virginia's proposal formed the basis for the ten amendments to the Constitution—The Bill of Rights—that were appended in 1791, just one year before Mason's death.
35. Seat – a country estate or mansion.
36. A manor known as Gunston Hall belonged to the Fowke family in Brewood Parish, Staffordshire, England. Gerard Fowke used the name also at his seat in Charles County, Maryland. See Helen Hill Miler, *George Mason, Gentleman* Revolutionary (Chapel Hill: The University of North Carolina Press, 1975), 56.
37. George Mason VI (1786–1834) inherited Gunston Hall and it was in the possession of his widow in 1839. He was the son of George Mason V of Lexington, and grandson of George Mason IV of Gunston Hall.
38. The imposing avenue of four rows of cherry trees George Mason planted enhanced a vista for the approaching visitor making the trees "seem to approach as they recede." Mason utilized elements of perspective common in landscaping ideas in ordered English and French design that created avenues of trees making the house the focal point of the vista. Such ideas regarding avenues were available in eighteenth century publications including *The Nobleman, Gentleman, and Gardener's Recreation: or, an Introduction to Gardening....* by Stephen Switzer (London, 1715) and John Evelyn's *Sylva, or a Discourse of Forest-Trees...* (London, 1679). Both these volumes were in the library of John Mercer, George Mason's uncle and his guardian after 1735, and would likely have been accessible to Mason as a young man.

    However, Mason's "magic" or trick of the eye where an unsuspecting guest standing at the center of the doorway and looking back at the avenue would only see four trees until moving off center, appears to be an unusual horticultural feature in colonial American gardens. Further, the optical illusion Mason achieved is not one suggested in contemporary horticultural literature. Whatever the source of his idea, Mason's design was carefully conceived and planned, growing the trees from seed and grooming them over years of time. John Mason records his father's great pleasure in displaying the "magic" concealed within the avenue and reveals the subtle and complex nature of George Mason's humor. Personal conversations: Gordon Chappell, Director of Landscape and Facilities Service, Colonial Williamsburg Foundation, Williamsburg, VA; Kent Brinkley, Horticulturalist,

Colonial Williamsburg Foundation; and William Myer, Horticulturalist, Gunston Hall Plantation, Mason Neck, VA.

39. Pettiauger or periagua/piragua is an Anglicised version of the French word pirogue, meaning a Carib dugout boat. Pettiaguers were multiple-log vessels, common along the Carolina coastline and the Chesapeake region of Virginia by the eighteenth century. Generally built by slaves and manned by black oarsmen, these rugged and sturdy boats were used to transport goods and lumber, holding as much as eighty or a hundred barrels. John Michael Vlach, *The Afro-American Tradition in Decorative Arts* (Cleveland: The Cleveland Museum of Art, 1978), 97–107; also personal conversation with John Sands, Director of Collections and Conservation, Colonial Williamsburg Foundation, Williamsburg, VA.
40. Janus, a thoroughbred, English stallion, foaled in 1746, was purchased by Gloucester County planter Mordacai Booth and imported from London in 1756. Said to be a "remarkable Horse" of great speed, Janus influenced the development of the American thoroughbred sprinter and modern quarter horse. A *Virginia Gazette* advertisement in 1777 offered for sale a four year old colt sired by Janus, "famous for begetting the finest horses for the harness or saddle." Alexander Mackay-Smith, *The Colonial Quarter Race Horse* (Richmond, VA: Press of Whittet and Shepperson, 1983), 102–133.
41. The four plantations or quarters included Occoquan, Dogue Neck, Hallowing Point, and Pohick Quarter, in addition to Gunston Hall on this tract of about 5500 acres on Mason Neck.
42. Although wheat was not a principal export crop in the eighteenth century, Mason and others were shipping quantities abroad for profit. In July 1789, George Mason shipped thirteen hogsheads—large barrels holding 1000 lbs. or more—of tobacco (over 13,000 lbs. total) and 1289 bushels of wheat to Bordeaux, France on the ship *Becky* to John Mason's company, Fenwick & Mason. George Mason requested that, "my Remittances are to remain to the Credit of my own Proper Account." Rutland, *Papers of George Mason*, pp. 1162, 1163. Numerous letters from these later years of Mason's life indicate that wheat was exported.
43. Mason kept no steward or manager for the estate.

Genealogy

George Mason I (1629–1686) m.
1. Mary French (? – after 1660)—George Mason II
2. Frances Norgrave

George Mason II (1660–1716) m.
1. Mary Fowke (?– c.1704)—George Mason III
2. Elizabeth Waugh (?–1707)
3. Sarah Taliaferro (? –1716)

George Mason III (1690–1735) m.
Ann Thomson (1699–1762)—George Mason IV

George Mason IV *of Gunston Hall* (1725–1792) m.
1. Ann Eilbeck (1734–1773)
2. Sarah Brent (1733?–1805?)

Children of George Mason IV and Ann Eilbeck Mason:

George Mason V (1753–1796) m. Elizabeth Mary Ann Barnes Hooe (1768–1814)
Ann "Nancy" Eilbeck Mason (1755–1814) m. Rinaldo Johnson (1755–1811)
William Mason (1756–1757)
William Mason (1757–1818) m. Ann Stuart (1770–1855)
Thomson Mason (1759–1820) m. Sarah McCarty Chichester (?–?)
Sarah "Sally" Eilbeck Mason (1760–1823) m. Daniel McCarty, Jr. (1758–1801)
Mary Thomson Mason (1762–1806) m. John Travers Cooke (1755–1819)
John Mason (1766–1849) m. Anna Maria Murray (1776–1859)
Elizabeth "Betsey" Mason (1768–before 1799) m. William Thornton (1758–1800)
Thomas Mason (1770–1800) m. Sarah Barnes Hooe (1769–1815)
James & Richard Mason (1772–1772)

The Virginia Declaration of Rights

[First Draft, ca. 20–26 May 1776]

A DECLARATION OF RIGHTS, made by the Representatives of the good People of Virginia, assembled in full Convention; and recommended to Posterity as the Basis and Foundation of Government.

That all Men are born equally free and independant [sic], and have certain inherent natural Rights, of which they can not [sic] by any Compact, deprive or divest their Posterity; among which are the Enjoyment of Life and Liberty, with the Means of acquiring and possessing Property, and pursueing [sic] and obtaining Happiness and Safety.

That Power is, by God and Nature, vested in, and consequently derived from the People; that Magistrates are their Trustees and Servants, and at all times amenable to them.

That Government is, or ought to be, instituted for the common Benefit and Security of the People, Nation, or Community. Of all the various Modes and Forms of Government, that is best, which is capable of producing the greatest Degree of Happiness and Safety, and is most effectually secured against the Danger of maladministration. And that whenever any Government shall be found inadequate, or contrary to these Purposes, a Majority of the Community had an indubitable, inalianable and indefeasible Right to reform, alter or abolish it, in such Manner as shall be judged most conducive to the Public Weal.

That no Man, or Set of Men are entitled to exclusive or seperate [sic]Emoluments or Privileges from the Community, but in Consideration of public Services; which not being descendible, or hereditary, the Idea of a Man born a Magistrate, a Legislator, or a Judge is unnatural and absurd.

That the legislative and executive Powers of the State shoud [sic] be separate and distinct from the judicative; and that the Members of the two first may be restraind [sic] from Oppression, by feeling and participating the Burthens they may lay upon the People; they should, at fixed Periods be reduced to a private Station, and returned, by frequent, certain and regular Elections, into that Body from which they were taken.

That no part of a Man's Property can be taken from him, or applied to public uses, without the Consent of himself, or his legal Representatives; nor are the People bound by any Laws, but such as they have in like Manner assented to for their common Good.

That in all capital or criminal Prosecutions, a Man hath a right to demand the Cause and Nature of his Accusation, to be confronted with the Accusers or Witnesses, to call for Evidence in his favour, and to a speedy Tryal by a Jury of his Vicinage; without whose unanimous Consent, he can not [sic] be found guilty; nor can he be compelled to give Evidence against himself. And that no Man, except in times of actual Invasion or Insurrection, can be imprisoned upon Suspicion of Crimes against the State, unsupported by Legal Evidence.

That no free Government, or the Blessings of Liberty can be preserved to any People, but by a firm adherence to Justice, Moderation, Temperance, Frugality, and Virtue and by frequent Recurrence to fundamental Principles.

That as Religion, or the Duty which we owe to our divine and omnipotent Creator, and the Manner of discharging it, can be governed only by Reason and Conviction, not by Force or Violence; and therefore that all Men shou'd enjoy the fullest Toleration in the Exercise of Religion, according to the Dictates of Conscience, unpunished and unrestrained by the Magistrate, unless, under Colour of Religion, any Man disturb the Peace, the Happiness, or Safety of Society, or of Individuals. And that it is the mutual Duty of all, to practice Christian Forbearance, Love and Charity towards Each other.

That in all controversies respecting Property, and in Suits between Man and Man, the ancient Tryal by Jury is preferable to any other, and ought to be held sacred.

That the freedom of the press, being the great bulwark of Liberty, can never be restrained but in a despotic government.

That laws having a retrospect [sic] to crimes, & punishing offences committed before the existence of such laws, are generally dangerous, and ought to be avoided.

N. B. It is proposed to make some alteration in this last article when reported to the house. Perhaps somewhat like the following

That all laws having a retrospect to crimes, & punishing offences committed before the existence of such laws are dangerous, and ought to be avoided, except in cases of great, & evident necessity, when safety of the state absolutely requires them. This is thought to state with more precision the doctrine respecting ex post facto laws & to signify to posterity that it is considered not so much as a law of right, as the great law of necessity, which by the well known maxim is – allowed to supersede all human institutions.

Another is agreed to in committee condemning the use of general warrants; & one other to prevent the suspension of laws, or the execution of them.

The above clauses, with some small alterations, & the addition of one, or two more, have already been agreed to in the Committee appointed to prepare a declaration of rights; when this business is finished in the house, the committee will proceed to the ordinance of government.

T. L. Lee

Written in George Mason's handwriting, except for the end portion beginning "That the freedom of the press..." which is in Thomas Ludwell Lee's hand. Original in the Library of Congress, Washington, D.C.

Mason's Objections to the Constitution

[Circa 16 September 1787]

THERE IS NO DECLARATION OF RIGHTS, and the Laws of the general Government being paramount to the Laws & Constitutions of the several States, the Declarations of Rights in the separate States are no Security. Nor are the People secured even in the Enjoyment of the Benefit of the common Law.

In the House of Representatives, there is not the Substance, but the Shadow only of Representation; which can never produce proper Information in the Legislature, or inspire Confidence in the People; the Laws will therefore be generally made by men little concern'd in, and unacquainted with their Effects and Consequences.

The Senate have the Power of altering all money Bills, and of originating appropriations of money, & the Sallerys [sic] of the Officers of their own Appointment, in Conjunction with the president of the United States; altho' they are not the Representatives of the People, or amenable to them.

These, with their other great Powers, (viz., their Power in the Appointment of Ambassadors and all public Officers, in making Treaties, and in trying all Impeachments) their Influence upon & Connection with the supreme Executive from these Causes, their Duration of Office, and their being a constant existing Body, almost continually sitting, joined with their being one complete Branch of the Legislature will destroy any Ballance [sic] in the Government, & enable them to accomplish what Usurpations they please upon the Rights and Liberty of the People.

The Judiciary of the United States is so constructed & extended, as to absorb and destroy the Judiciaries of the several States; thereby rendering Law as tedious[,] intricate and expensive, & Justice as unattainable, by a great Part of the Community, as in England, and enabling the Rich to oppress & ruin the Poor.

The President of the United States has no constitutional Council (a thing unknown in any safe & regular Government) he will therefore be unsupported by proper information and Advice; and will generally be directed by Minions and Favourites. Or he will become a Tool to the Senate—or a Council of State will grow out of the principal Officers of the great Departments; the worst & most dangerous of all Ingredients for such a Council, in a free country.

From this fatal Defect has arisen the improper Power of the Senate in the appointment of public Officers, and the alarming Dependence & Connection between that Branch of the Legislature and the supreme Executive.

Hence also sprung that unnecessary Officer, the Vice-President; who for want of other Employment, is made President of the Senate; thereby dangerously blending the executive and legislative Powers; besides always giving to some one of the States an unnecessary & unjust pre-eminence over the others.

The President of the United States has the unrestrained Power of granting Pardons for Treason; which may be sometimes exercised to screen from punishment those whom he had secretly instigated to commit the Crime, & thereby prevent a Discovery of his own Guilt.

By declaring all Treaties supreme Laws of the Land, the Executive & the Senate have in many Cases, an exclusive power of ligislation [sic]; which might have been avoided by proper Distinctions with respect to Treaties, and requiring the Assent of the House of Representatives, where it cou'd be done, with Safety.

By requiring only a Majority to make all commercial & Navigation Laws, the five Southern States (whose Produce & Circumstances are totally different from those of the eight northern and Eastern States) may be ruined; for such rigid & premature Regulations may be made, as will enable the Merchants of the northern & Eastern States not only to demand an exorbitant Freight, but to monopolize the Purchase of the Commodities at their own Price, for many Years; to the great Injury of the landed Interest, & Impoverishment of the People; and the Danger is the greater, as the Gain on one Side will be in Proportion to the Loss on the other. Whereas, requiring two thirds of the Members present in both Houses wou'd have produced mutual moderation, promoted the general Interest, and removed an insuperable Objection to the adoption of the Government.

Under their own Construction of the general Clause, at the End of the enumerated Powers, the Congress may grant Monopolies in Trade & Commerce, constitute new Crimes, inflict unusual and severe Punishments, & extend their Powers as far as they shall think proper; so that the State Legislatures have no Security for the Powers now presumed to remain to them, or the People for their Rights.

There is no Declaration of any kind, for preserving the Liberty of the Press, the Tryal by Jury in Civil Causes; nor against the Danger of standing Armys in time of Peace.

The State Legislatures are restrained from laying Import Duties on their own Produce.

Both the general Legislature* and the State Legislatures are expressly prohibited making ex post facto Laws; tho' there never was, nor can be a Legislature but must and will make such Laws, when Necessity and the public Safety require them; which will hereafter be a Breach of all the Constitutions in the Union, and afford precedents for other Innovations.

This government will set out a moderate Aristocracy: it is at present Impossible to foresee whether it will, in its operation, produce a Monarchy, or a corrupt tyrannical Aristocracy; it will most probably vibrate some years between the two, and then terminate in the one or the other.

**The general Legislature is restrained from prohibiting the further Importation of Slaves for twenty odd years; tho' such Importations render the United States weaker, more vulnerable, and less capable of Defense.*

Written in George Mason's handwriting on the back of the Committee of Style draft of the United States Constitution. Original in the Chapin Library, Williams College, Williamstown, MA.

Bibliography

Copeland, Pamela C. and Richard K. MacMaster. *The Five George Masons, Patriots and Planters of Virginia and Maryland*. Lorton, VA: The Board of Regents of Gunston Hall, 1989.

Miller, Helen Hill. *George Mason, Gentleman Revolutionary*. Chapel Hill: The University of North Carolina Press, 1975.

Rowland, Kate Mason. *The Life of George Mason*. New York. Russell & Russell, Inc., 1964.

Rutland, Robert A. *The Birth of the Bill of Rights*. Boston: Northeastern University Press, 1983.

———. *George Mason and the War for Independence*. Williamsburg, VA: Virginia Independence Bicentennial Commission, 1976.

———. *George Mason, Reluctant Statesman*. Baton Rouge: Louisiana State University Press, 1961.

———. *The Papers of George Mason*. Chapel Hill: The University Press of North Carolina, 1970.

Index

Gunston Hall

Gunston Hall is now a historic site open to the public. Built between 1755 and 1759, Gunston Hall is as famous for its architecture as for its association with patriot and planter George Mason. The house, once a focal point of a 5,500 acre plantation, is located on the Potomac River about eight miles south of Mount Vernon, the estate of Mason's neighbor and long-time friend, George Washington. During Mason's lifetime, the property was home and workplace to a community of over 100 people, the majority of them enslaved African Americans. Situated only four miles from the main north-south road (what is now U.S. Route 1), Gunston Hall was a stopping place for many visitors, including Thomas Jefferson, James Madison, James Monroe, and other patriots who came to discuss the politics of revolution and nation building with George Mason.

Today Gunston Hall encompasses 550 acres of Mason's original tract and features extensive grounds, reconstructed outbuildings, a one mile nature trail to the Potomac River, the Mason family burial ground, and a Visitor's Center featuring an orientation film, exhibits, and a museum shop. The modest Georgian exterior of Gunston Hall is typical of eighteenth century domestic architecture in the Chesapeake region, while the interior reflects some of the most magnificently ornamented rooms of the Colonial period, attributed to two talented English craftsmen, William Buckland and William Bernard Sears.

Owned and operated by the Commonwealth of Virginia and administered by the Board of Regents of The National Society of The Colonial Dames of America, Gunston Hall offers daily tours as well as rental facilities for private and corporate functions. For further information, check the website or contact Gunston Hall.

GUNSTON HALL
10709 Gunston Road, Mason Neck, Virginia 22079-3901
Phone: (703)550-9220 • FAX: (703)550-9480
E-mail: historic@gunstonhall.org • Website: www.gunstonhall.org

About the Editor

TERRY K. DUNN brought her long experience as a teacher, historical researcher, and museum interpreter at Gunston Hall and Colonial Williamsburg to the editing of this work. She holds a B. S. in Zoology from Penn State and an M. A. in American History from George Mason University. Terry lives in Williamsburg, Virginia with her husband, Keith, her father, Leonard, a cockatoo, a parrot, and a beagle.

CPSIA information can be obtained
at www.ICGtesting.com
Printed in the USA
LVIW011247290912
300857LV00004B